Sencha MVC A

A practical guide for designers and developers to create
scalable enterprise-class web applications in ExtJS and
Sencha Touch using the Sencha MVC architecture

Ajit Kumar

PUBLISHING

BIRMINGHAM - MUMBAI

Sencha MVC Architecture

First published: November 2012

Production Reference: 1011112

Published by Packt Publishing Ltd.
Livery Place
35 Livery Street
Birmingham B3 2PB, UK.

ISBN 978-1-84951-888-8

www.packtpub.com

Cover Image by Asher Wishkerman (wishkerman@hotmail.com)

Credits

Author
Ajit Kumar

Reviewers
Dave Kinsella

Deepak Vohra

Acquisition Editor
Usha Iyer

Commissioning Editor
Meeta Rajani

Technical Editors
Rohit Rajgor

Nitee Shetty

Copy Editor
Alfida Paiva

Project Coordinator
Michelle Quadros

Proofreader
Maria Gould

Indexer
Hemangini Bari

Graphics
Aditi Gajjar

Valentina Dsilva

Production Coordinator
Melwyn D'sa

Cover Work
Melwyn D'sa

About the Author

Ajit Kumar started his IT career with Honeywell, Bangalore in the field of embedded systems and moved on to enterprise business applications (such as ERP) in his 12 year career. From day one, he has been a staunch supporter and promoter of Open Source and believes strongly that Open Source is the way for a liberal, diversified, and democratic setup, like India.

He dreams and continuously endeavors that the architecture, frameworks, and tools facilitate the software development at the speed of thought.

He has done his B.E. in Computer Science and Engineering from the Bihar Institute of Technology and co-founded Walking Tree, which is based out of Hyderabad, India. Here he plays the role of CTO and works on fulfilling his vision.

I would like to thank my wife, Priti, and my sons, Pratyush and Piyush, for their support and encouragement, and all the people behind the Sencha products and other Open Source projects.

About the Reviewers

Dave Kinsella has been a professional web developer since 1996. Over the years, he has worked with many different technologies on projects ranging from public websites and web applications to large intranet content management systems. He has never considered himself to be a specialist in any particular field other than the general topic of "Web Technology" and spends a lot of his spare time trying out new ideas and techniques. Many of these can be found on his blog: webdeveloper2.com.

He is currently employed by Quantiv Limited as the Head of Interactive Design, where he is designing and building flexible web-based interfaces for complex data-processing applications using ExtJS and Sencha Touch.

Deepak Vohra is a consultant and a principal member of the NuBean.com software company. He is a Sun Certified Java Programmer and Web Component Developer, and has worked in the fields of XML and Java programming and J2EE for over five years. He is the co-author of the book *Pro XML Development with Java Technology, Apress* and was the technical reviewer for the book *WebLogic: The Definitive Guide, O'Reilly* . He was also the technical reviewer for the book *Ruby Programming for the Absolute Beginner, Course Technology PTR* and the technical editor for the book *Prototype and Scriptaculous in Action, Manning Publications*. He is also the author of the Packt Publishing books *JDBC 4.0 and Oracle JDeveloper for J2EE Development, Processing XML documents with Oracle JDeveloper 11g*, and *EJB 3.0 Database Persistence with Oracle Fusion Middleware 11g*.

www.PacktPub.com

Support files, eBooks, discount offers and more

You might want to visit www.PacktPub.com for support files and downloads related to your book.

Did you know that Packt offers eBook versions of every book published, with PDF and ePub files available? You can upgrade to the eBook version at www.PacktPub.com and as a print book customer, you are entitled to a discount on the eBook copy. Get in touch with us at service@packtpub.com for more details.

At www.PacktPub.com, you can also read a collection of free technical articles, sign up for a range of free newsletters and receive exclusive discounts and offers on Packt books and eBooks.

http://PacktLib.PacktPub.com

Do you need instant solutions to your IT questions? PacktLib is Pack's online digital book library. Here, you can access, read and search across Pack's entire library of books.

Why Subscribe?

- Fully searchable across every book published by Packt
- Copy and paste, print and bookmark content
- On demand and accessible via web browser

Free Access for Packt account holders

If you have an account with Packt at www.PacktPub.com, you can use this to access PacktLib today and view nine entirely free books. Simply use your login credentials for immediate access.

Table of Contents

Preface	**1**
Chapter 1: Sencha MVC Architecture	**7**
Why Client-side MVC architecture	**10**
Why Sencha MVC architecture	**12**
Sencha MVC architecture	**18**
Ext JS 4.1	20
Sencha Touch	21
Summary	**22**
Chapter 2: Creating an Application	**23**
Application design	**25**
ExtJS-based application	27
Folder structure	27
Sencha Touch-based application	41
Folder structure	42
Summary	**55**
Chapter 3: Building Blocks	**57**
Model	**58**
Store	61
View	**64**
Controller	**65**
ExtJS	65
Sencha Touch	65
Profile	66
Application	**68**
Ext JS	69
Sencha Touch	69
Routing and history	**70**
Dependency management with loader	**71**
Summary	**72**

Chapter 4: Class System   73

Class system   74
Naming convention   78
    Class   78
    File   79
    Methods and variables   79
    Properties   79
Defining a class   80
    Configuration   80
Alias   82
Alternate class name   83
Extend   83
Statics   84
    Inheritable statics   84
Mixin   85
Singleton   87
    Uses versus requires   88
Error reporting   90

Class loader   91
Asynchronous loading   92
Synchronous loading   92
Hybrid loading   93

Summary   93

Chapter 5: Challenges and Solutions   95

Challenges   95
Project creation   95
Debugging   95
Build   96
Minification   98

Solutions   98
Project creation   98
Debugging   101
    User <script> tag   101
    Disable caching for loader   102
Build   103
Minification   108

Summary   108

Index   109

Preface

Model-View-Controller is a popular architecture among the software developers to build scalable and maintainable applications. While most of the time we use the server-side MVC architecture, with the complexity increasing in the Rich Application Development, a similar architecture is needed on the client-side, as well. The client-side MVC architecture allows us to de-couple the presentation from the model and the controller logic. The newly introduced client-side MVC architecture in Sencha's two frameworks — ExtJS and Touch — offers a great way to model applications where we can leverage the benefits of the architecture, and also with the Sencha SDK Tools we can manage the complete project — from creation to build and packaging — effectively. This, on one side, helps us to develop an application by following the MVC architectural principles, project structure, and coding guidelines while, on the other side, it optimizes our build and packaging for the Web.

What this book covers

Chapter 1, Sencha MVC Architecture: This chapter describes the MVC architecture and outlines the need of having an MVC architecture implemented on the clientside, which runs inside a browser. The chapter shows how to model an application without using Sencha MVC architecture and look at the demerits of that modeling. It then reviews the benefits that one can get by following Sencha MVC architecture. Subsequently, it visits the classes in ExtJS as well as Sencha Touch, which map to the model, view, and controller.

Chapter 2, Creating an Application: In this chapter we look at a sample application and learn how to model it as per the MVC architecture and map the different building blocks to the classes provided by ExtJS and Sencha Touch. The application development involves how to identify the views, models, and controllers in an application, how to make use of multiple controllers within an application and pass the data and control between them to achieve the overall application behavior. At the end, we look at some of the rules related to class naming convention, folder structure, and so on, which is required to get the application up and running.

Chapter 3, Building Blocks: This chapter covers the different classes, which are part of the MVC architecture in ExtJS as well as Sencha Touch. It covers the function of each of these classes and the differences in their behavior and usage. In addition to the common classes—Application, Controller, Model, View (Component)—it also covers the Touch-specific way to handle profiles to encapsulate device-specific behaviors and layout in the applications. Also, it shows how to set up the routes in Touch application and have the history tracking in place.

Chapter 4, Class System: This chapter explains how the new class system works and what are the functionalities offered by the class system. It also covers what are the naming conventions put in place and recommended by the framework, how to define classes, set up dependencies, implement inheritance, enhance capability using mixins, create singleton classes, and so on.

Chapter 5, Challenges and Solutions: This chapter reviews some of the main challenges when it comes to developing an MVC-based application – project creation, build, debugging, and packaging. With the challenges at hand, the chapter then covers the Sencha SDK Tools to show how this tool can help us address each of those challenges.

What you need for this book

To run the examples in this book you will need the following software:

- Eclipse 3.3 or above with JEE (for example, Helios) and JavaScript (JSDT) support
- Oracle Java JDK 1.5 or above
- ExtJS 4.1 library
- Sencha Touch 2.0 library
- Android SDK
- ADT Plug-in
- Apache Tomcat 6.0 or above

Who this book is for

This book is for someone who wants to understand the Sencha ExtJS and Touch frameworks, in general, and the Sencha MVC Architecture, in specific, to create scalable and maintainable applications. The book provides a complete end-to-end implementation of an application using the Sencha ExtJS as well as Sencha Touch frameworks by applying the Sencha MVC Architecture. The book is also useful for someone who wants to understand how the Sencha SDK Tools work and how one can set up an effective project management through project setup and build management.

Conventions

In this book, you will find a number of styles of text that distinguish between different kinds of information. Here are some examples of these styles, and an explanation of their meaning.

Code words in text are shown as follows: "Profile functionality is offered by the `Ext.app.Profile` class."

A block of code is set as follows:

```
{
  success: true,
  users: [
    {id: 1, name: 'Sunil',  email: 'sunil@wtc.com'},
    {id: 2, name: 'Sujit', email: 'sujit@wtc.com'},
    {id: 3, name: 'Alok', email: 'alok@wtc.com'},
    {id: 4, name: 'Pradeep', email: 'pradeep@wtc.com'},
    {id: 5, name: 'Ajit', email: 'ajit@wtc.com'}
  ]
}
```

New terms and **important words** are shown in bold. Words that you see on the screen, in menus or dialog boxes for example, appear in the text like this: "Create a **Dynamic Web Project** workspace in Eclipse".

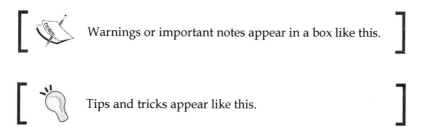

Warnings or important notes appear in a box like this.

Tips and tricks appear like this.

Reader feedback

Feedback from our readers is always welcome. Let us know what you think about this book—what you liked or may have disliked. Reader feedback is important for us to develop titles that you really get the most out of.

To send us general feedback, simply send an e-mail to feedback@packtpub.com, and mention the book title through the subject of your message.

If there is a topic that you have expertise in and you are interested in either writing or contributing to a book, see our author guide on www.packtpub.com/authors.

Customer support

Now that you are the proud owner of a Packt book, we have a number of things to help you to get the most from your purchase.

Downloading the example code

You can download the example code files for all Packt books you have purchased from your account at http://www.packtpub.com. If you purchased this book elsewhere, you can visit http://www.packtpub.com/support and register to have the files e-mailed directly to you.

Errata

Although we have taken every care to ensure the accuracy of our content, mistakes do happen. If you find a mistake in one of our books—maybe a mistake in the text or the code—we would be grateful if you would report this to us. By doing so, you can save other readers from frustration and help us improve subsequent versions of this book. If you find any errata, please report them by visiting http://www.packtpub.com/support, selecting your book, clicking on the **errata submission form** link, and entering the details of your errata. Once your errata are verified, your submission will be accepted and the errata will be uploaded to our website, or added to any list of existing errata, under the Errata section of that title.

Piracy

Piracy of copyright material on the Internet is an ongoing problem across all media. At Packt, we take the protection of our copyright and licenses very seriously. If you come across any illegal copies of our works, in any form, on the Internet, please provide us with the location address or website name immediately so that we can pursue a remedy.

Please contact us at copyright@packtpub.com with a link to the suspected pirated material.

We appreciate your help in protecting our authors, and our ability to bring you valuable content.

Questions

You can contact us at questions@packtpub.com if you are having a problem with any aspect of the book, and we will do our best to address it.

1
Sencha MVC Architecture

MVC architecture is a well-known and a famous architecture. In an application, if there is a view (for example, a form to create payment into a system) and a user would use it to interact with the system, MVC architecture comes as the default and preferred architecture. It is the favorite architecture to model our application so that the presentation logic can be separated from the business logic. In this chapter, we will look at the MVC architecture in general, and understand how it is mapped to Sencha MVC Architecture.

In this, and the subsequent chapters, we will be demonstrating the concepts using some functional code for which the following softwares are required:

- Eclipse 3.3 or above with JEE (for example, Helios) and JavaScript (JSDT) support
- Oracle Java JDK 1.5 or above
- Ext JS 4.1 library
- Sencha Touch 2.0 library
- Android SDK
- ADT plugin
- Apache Tomcat 6.0 or above

Before we get any further, we would need a development environment to be set up, so that we are able to build, deploy, and test the application. For brevity, we will not be covering how to set up the development environment in detail. The following are the high-level steps to get the project set up:

1. Create a **Dynamic Web Project** workspace in Eclipse.
2. Create a **ch01** folder under **WebContent** where we will be keeping the code related to this chapter.

Downloading the example code

You can download the example code files for all Packt books you have purchased from your account at http://www.packtpub.com . If you purchased this book elsewhere, you can visit http://www. packtpub.com/support and register to have the files e-mailed directly to you.

After creation, your project should look as shown in the following screenshot:

3. In Eclipse, go to **Window | Preferences**.

4. Expand **Server**, go to **Server Runtime Environments**, and add an entry for Apache Tomcat shown as follows:

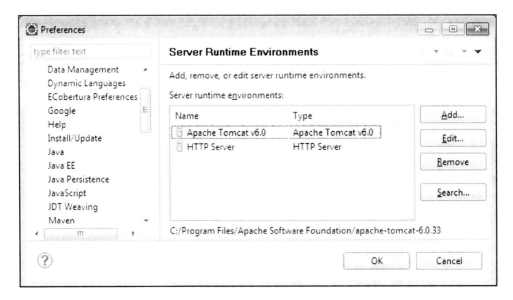

5. Go to the **Servers** perspective and add **SenchaArchitectureBook** to the **Configured** list, shown as follows:

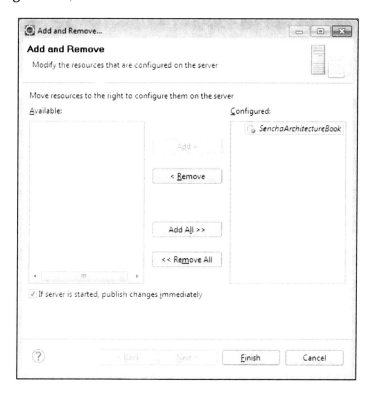

6. Now you will be able to publish and start the server to see that the project is deployed successfully. You should be able to access the `http://<host>:<port>/SenchaArchitectureBook/` URL to access the application.

Throughout this book, for the parts referring to Sencha Touch, we will be using the WebKit browsers, for example, Chrome and Safari, on the desktop to demonstrate the concepts. However, if you intend to test them on the real device, the steps would be more involved ones and you can refer to *Chapter 1, Gear up for the Journey* from the book *Sencha Touch Cookbook, Packt Publishing*, for detailed steps to set up the environment for Android, iOS, and Blackberry devices. Also, the book assumes that you have done some level of Ext JS or Sencha Touch development and are aware of the components and the programming model of Sencha.

Why Client-side MVC architecture

The MVC architecture is all about organizing the code in the form of models, views, and controllers. Models maintain the state of the application, views take care of the presentation of the application state, and controllers provide the much needed functionality to handle the user action and carry out the business logic execution as part of it, which changes the application state. The complete interaction between the pieces — model, view, and controller — is depicted in the following diagram. The solid lines show the flow of logic in terms of method invocation, whereas the dotted lines show the flow of events:

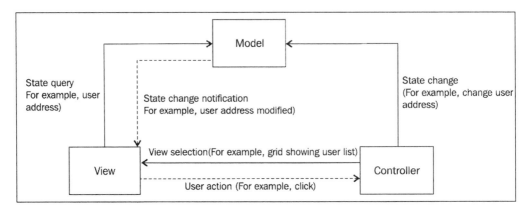

The previous diagram depicts the holistic view of the MVC architecture and how the different pieces of the architecture interact with each other in order to address the specific goals that the architecture promises to address. In this book, we do not intend to redefine and explain the complete MVC architecture. However, you may read more about the architecture at http://en.wikipedia.org/wiki/Model%E2%80 %93view%E2%80%93controller.

Traditionally, in a web application, MVC architecture has been implemented on the server side to keep the view logic away from the business logic. In a typical web application, the server side code is structured in the form of model-view-controller to benefit from the structure to make the application more maintainable, allow parallel development, align the application with the Progressive Enhancement goals, and so on. In this case, the view code takes care of sending the (X)HTML, CSS, and JavaScript to the browser as part of the response in order to show the desired view to the user (for example, a grid showing a list of users with a button to edit the user address). The browser renders the HTML to show the content using the mentioned HTML tags (for example, a <table> tag to show the users list), uses CSS to style the content (for example, show the alternate rows with a different color), and uses

JavaScript to add interactivity to the view and take care of the behavior (for example, on clicking the **Edit** button, showing a form to edit the user address). This has been depicted in the following diagram where the complete MVC is implemented on the server side, whereas on the browser side, JavaScript, CSS, and HTML is used:

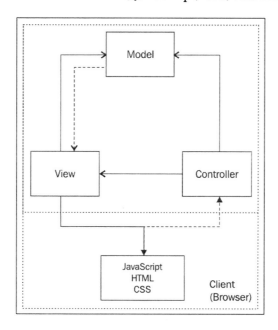

Implementation of the previous architecture cleans up the server-side code. However, the browser-side code remains very messy with the HTML, CSS, and JavaScript intermixed. This gets multiplied when a considerable amount of code is written to run inside the browser, to render the view, and handle the interactions with the user, for example, as in **Rich Internet Applications (RIA)**. In addition to that, given the flexibility JavaScript offers, it makes the matter worse where people do things such as use the variables without defining them, and write functions and use them without worrying about writing object-oriented JavaScript. The need for the code that runs inside the browser does not differ much from the one that runs on the server side, hence the development principles (maintainability, reusability, and so on), which apply to the server-side code, also apply to the browser-side code. HTML and CSS form the view, JavaScript becomes the controller, and the objects, containing the state of the UI, form the model.

Effectively, there is a need to have two MVC patterns in the application, one on the browser side and the other on the server side, to reap the complete benefit of the architecture. The following diagram depicts browser-side MVC architecture and how it would interface with the server-side MVC:

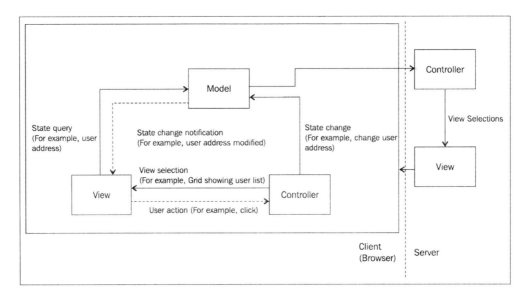

View is the code that produces and renders HTML tags and applies CSS to them (for example, producing the `<table>` tag to show the users list with the alternate rows highlighted with a different color). Model contains the state of the application (for example, the list of users with their address details) in the form of one or more JavaScript objects/variables. Controller is a part of JavaScript taking care of the behavior part of the UI (for example, the `onclick` handler of the `Edit` button). Cache usually maintains the collection of models and provides a convenient way for the browser-side application to fetch the state and state information.

Why Sencha MVC architecture

Now that we understand the need of having MVC architecture on the client side, let us see why the Sencha MVC architecture was introduced as part of the Sencha Ext JS and Touch frameworks.

Let us look at the following code, written using Ext JS, which shows the list of users (from a `users.json` file) and shows an **Edit User** window with a form, populated with the selected record detail, when an entry in the list is double-clicked:

```
Ext.onReady(function() {

  //Define the user model
  Ext.define('User', {
    extend : 'Ext.data.Model',
    fields : [ 'id', 'name', 'email'],
  });

  //Define the Users store, which uses the User as the model
  //and loads models from the users.json file
  Ext.define('Users', {
    extend : 'Ext.data.Store',
    model : 'User',
    autoLoad : true,    //load the data into the store as soon as it
is initialized

    //proxy configuration, which is used to load the data
    proxy : {
      type : 'ajax',
      api : {
        read : 'data/users.json'
      },
      reader : {
        type : 'json',
        root : 'users',
        successProperty : 'success'
      }
    }
  });

  //Create an instance of the store that we defined above
  var store = Ext.create('Users', {});

  //Create the viewport which shows a grid loaded with the
  //user information from the store
  Ext.create('Ext.container.Viewport', {
    items : [ {
      xtype : 'grid',
      title : 'All Users',
      store : store,
```

```
columns : [ {
  header : 'Name',
  dataIndex : 'name',
  flex : 1
}, {
  header : 'Email',
  dataIndex : 'email',
  flex : 1
} ],
//event handlers
listeners : {
  itemdblclick : function(view, record) {

    //Create a window and show a form panel with the values
    //populated from the record
    var win = Ext.create('Ext.window.Window', {
      title : 'Edit User',
      layout: 'fit',
      autoShow: true,
      height: 120,
      width: 280,
      items: [{
        xtype: 'form',
        padding: '5 5 0 5',
        border: false,
        style: 'background-color: #fff;',
        items: [
          {
            xtype: 'textfield',
            name : 'name',
            fieldLabel: 'Name'
          },
          {
            xtype: 'textfield',
            name : 'email',
            fieldLabel: 'Email'
          }
        ]
      }],
      buttons: [{
        text: 'Save',
        action: 'save',
        handler: function() {
          alert('Save!');
```

```
                    }
                 },
                 {
                     text: 'Cancel',
                     action: 'cancel',
                     handler: function() {
                      alert('Cancel!');
                     }
                }]
            });

            win.show();
            win.down('form').loadRecord(record);
        }
      }
   } ]
  });

});
```

The example uses a `users.json` file, which has the following content:

```
{
  success: true,
  users: [
    {id: 1, name: 'Sunil',  email: 'sunil@wtc.com'},
    {id: 2, name: 'Sujit', email: 'sujit@wtc.com'},
    {id: 3, name: 'Alok', email: 'alok@wtc.com'},
    {id: 4, name: 'Pradeep', email: 'pradeep@wtc.com'},
    {id: 5, name: 'Ajit', email: 'ajit@wtc.com'}
  ]
}
```

`Ext.onReady` acts as the entry point to the application and is called as soon as the Ext JS framework is loaded and initialized. In the previous code, the complete application logic is written inside a single file, say, `app.js`. To run the code, we would create an `index.html` with the following content:

```
<html>
<head>
  <meta http-equiv="Content-Type" content="text/html; charset=utf-8">
  <title id="page-title">Account Manager</title>

  <link rel="stylesheet" type="text/css" href="<extjs folder>/
resources/css/ext-all.css">
```

```
   <script type="text/javascript" src="<extjs folder>/ext-all-debug.
js"></script>

   <script type="text/javascript" src="app.js"></script>
</head>
<body>

</body>
</html>
```

Replace `<extjs folder>` with the folder on your system where Ext JS 4 distribution was extracted. In my case, I kept it inside the **ch01** folder. The following screenshot shows what the project structure will look like after all the files are created:

Publish and **Start** the server and access the `http://<host>:<port>/` `SenchaArchitectureBook/ch01/index.html` URL from your browser. You will see the users' list and when you double-click on an entry, you will see the output as shown in the following screenshot:

Now, let us review the code and understand, though it is a functional code and meets the requirement, why it is considered to be a bad application. There can be multiple ways to model this application with a varied number of files making use of the various object-oriented principles. However, I have presented the worst (well, still not "the worst") way to code the application to help us understand the demerits and then see how each one of them can be addressed by sticking to a well-defined architecture. In the previous code, we first defined a `User` model with their fields, which is used by the store to represent the data in memory. Then we defined a `Users` store, linking the `User` model with it. In the store, we specified the `proxy` information, which the store would use to load the data from the mentioned URL, `data/users.json`. We then created a viewport to which we added a grid panel, `xtype: 'grid'`. This grid panel uses the instance of the `Users` store that we created using `var store = Ext.create('Users', {});`. The grid shows two columns, `Name` and `Email`. We also registered the handler for the `itemdblclick` event on the grid panel. The handler code creates a window with a form panel inside it and two buttons, **Save** and **Cancel**. We registered the dummy handlers for the **Save** and **Cancel** buttons, which show an alert message when the user clicks on them. We then show the window to the user and load the form inside it with the model that we had received from the framework as the second parameter to the `itemdblclick` handler.

If we look more closely, the following issues are evident in the previous way of coding the application:

1. If the grid has to be replaced with a different view component, say, a `DataView` component, the complete `app.js` code needs to be changed. For that matter, if any change is made to the view, model logic, and controller logic, then the `app.js` file needs to be modified, which makes the parallel development unmanageable in bigger projects.

2. Reusability of the view is not possible. Also, reusability of the model and controller logic is questionable.

3. Any change adds considerable testing effort as the testability of the code is really low. For example, if we choose to replace the grid with a data view component, then the complete code needs to be tested as the view logic is not separate from the controller.

4. A person working on this project will only understand the project structure, how the code flows, and where what is written, and it takes a lot of training and documentation to make a newcomer (to the project) understand the project and the code even though the person has the technical skill. A person working on this project will have the same challenge if he/she has to move to a different Ext JS/Touch project in the organization.

5. As the code structure does not follow any architectural guideline and best practices, for every project, a custom build process has to be developed and implemented for the build and packaging.

Until Ext JS 3.x, there was no MVC architecture. However, it was realized that given the rich functionality the framework offers, it was easy for people to divert from the best practices in a typical application development and introduce the problems that we outlined previously. The need was felt to have functionality in the framework, which enforces MVC architecture when it comes to application modeling and development. The benefits include the following:

- As long as the applications follow the architecture, they work the same way, and hence it becomes a lot easier for anyone who knows one application, to understand and follow all the applications following the same architecture.

- Sharing the code (view, controller logic, model and so on) across the applications becomes easier as all the projects follow the same folder structure, naming convention, and design, and hence a view written for one application can be used in another application.

- Making the changes becomes a lot more manageable and reduces the overall testing effort considerably.

- The Sencha MVC architecture uses class loading internally, which saves us from including all the JS files in the `index.html` and managing their orders manually. This comes as a great benefit to a medium to large application as there may be tens or hundreds of files.

- We can use Ext JS build tools to create standard and optimized versions of your applications for production use.

In the next chapter, we will look at modeling the same application (or a slightly enhanced one) using the Sencha MVC architecture.

Sencha MVC architecture

In the previous section, we discussed about the need to have an MVC architecture implemented on the browser side. Given that Sencha Ext JS and Touch are Rich Internet Application (RIA) frameworks having various components such as grid, chart, and combo-box, which use a collection of models and components such as form panel, which uses a model, these components have been designed in such a way that a collection of models can be shared across them. For example, user list can be shown in a grid or in a combo-box. Sencha Ext JS/Touch introduces a cache of models, called store, which is shared between the components. A model or a store interacts with the server-side controllers. The following diagram depicts the architecture used in Sencha Ext JS/Touch:

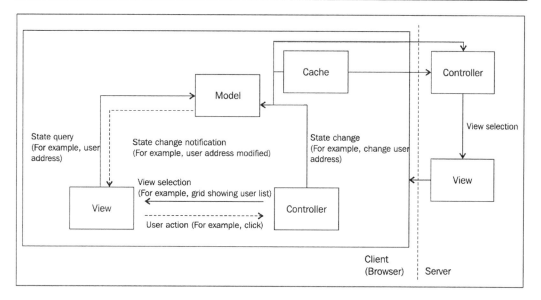

- Model is a collection of fields and their data. Models know how to persist themselves through the data package.
- View is any type of component. Grids, trees, and panels are all views.
- Controllers are special places to put all of the code that makes our application work.
- Store acts as a cache, which contains a collection of models.

For example, our application is supposed to display the list of users, a `User` model will represent the fields, such as `firstName`, `lastName`, and `address`. A `Users` store will contain a collection of `User` models. A grid panel represents the view to show a nicely styled users' list. Controller will handle the events such as a double-click on the grid row to show a form to edit a user's information, or click on the **Edit** button to edit the details of a user's address.

Now, on the basis of the framework, we will see how the MVC architecture is mapped.

Ext JS 4.1

Ext JS framework introduced MVC in Version 4.0 for the first time. It shares a lot of common code with the Touch framework. However, there are certain subtle differences which we will see in the subsequent chapters. Since its introduction, various cleanups and fine-tuning have been done to make it consistent and efficient. The framework provides various classes, as shown in the following diagram, to help us build a true MVC-based application:

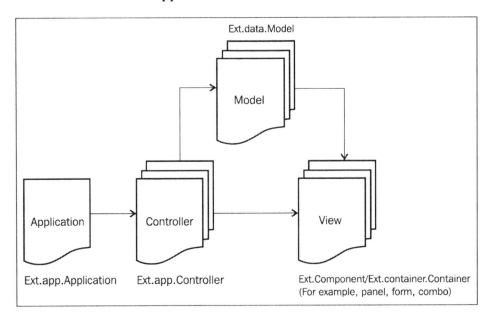

Ext.app.Application acts as the entry point in the MVC-based application. Use of this replaces the usage of the Ext.onReady method that is used to implement the entry point. Besides providing the entry point, the application also requires us to provide the dependencies in the form of controllers, which form the application, the stores, and so on. Controller, which extends Ext.app.Controller class, lists out the views and models that it will interact with. Based on the specified dependencies, the application loads the controller, which in turn loads the views and models and works with them to provide the desired view and allow the user to interact with it. Views are mainly the framework-defined visual components such as grid panel, form panel, tree panel, and buttons, or the user-defined components. In general, Ext.Component and Ext.container.Container are the base classes any view component extends to. Ext.data.Model is the base model class to define a model using the framework.

This object is used across various components to provide the application state. In addition to the models, the framework also offers a caching for the models in the form of the `Ext.data.Store` class, which can be passed to different components, such as grid, tree, and combo box, to show the data.

In *Chapter 2, Creating an Application*, we will discuss in detail each of these pieces.

Sencha Touch

As mentioned in the previous section, Sencha Touch is the foundation for MVC architecture. It was first implemented as part of it and later introduced to the Ext JS framework, as well. Similar to Ext JS, Sencha Touch supports `Ext.app.Application`, `Ext.app.Controller`, `Ext.Component`, `Ext.Container`, and `Ext.data.Model`, and they provide a similar set of functionality. However, there is an additional functionality called profiles, which is unique to the Touch framework. It allows us to define different profiles for different target devices (iPhone, iPad, Android phone, and so on). The profile functionality is offered by the `Ext.app.Profile` class and it consists of a collection of one or more controllers, one or more views, and one or more models. The `Application` class detects the profile applicable to the target device on which it is running and based on that, loads and initializes the respective controllers, models, and views. Store is available in Touch as well, and contains a collection of models. The following diagram depicts the components of the application architecture in Sencha Touch.

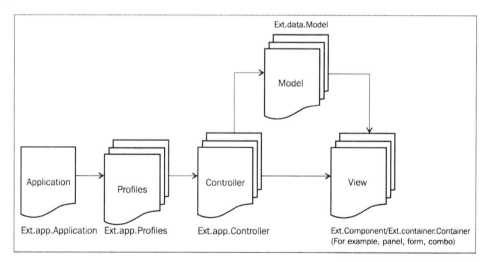

Summary

In this chapter, we looked at the MVC architecture and outlined the needs of having an MVC architecture implemented on the client side, which runs inside a browser. We then went on to see how we could have modeled our application without using Sencha MVC architecture and looked at the demerits of that modeling. We then looked at the benefits that one can get by following Sencha MVC architecture. Subsequently, we looked at the classes in Ext JS as well as Sencha Touch, which map to the model, view, and controller. In the following chapters, we will delve deeper into the specifics of the Sencha MVC architecture where we will see how to create an application using the Sencha MVC Architecture.

2
Creating an Application

In the previous chapter, we looked at the Sencha MVC architecture and also listed the various framework classes which map to the model-view-controller. In this chapter we will take a step-by-step approach to create a functional application in ExtJS as well as Sencha Touch, using the MVC architecture and the framework classes related to it. For the sake of completeness and illustration of the concepts, we will be taking up an application requirement and implementing it in ExtJS and Sencha Touch. Though most of the features are common in ExtJS and Touch, there are features such as profiles which are unique to Touch. In this chapter, we will cover the common functionality across the two frameworks and visit the specific features in the subsequent chapters.

As a requirement, we will be creating an application, which would:

- Show the list of departments and the users
- Show the list of users for a selected department
- Allow the user to edit user information
- Refresh the users list to get all the users of all the departments

The following screenshot shows the layout of the page we would like to have when the application is run:

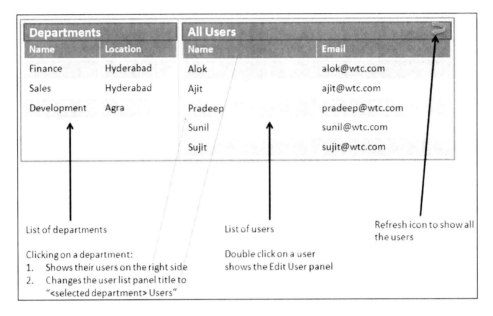

The following screenshot depicts the **Edit User** panel, which would show the field values populated from the selected user's record and allow the user to modify them:

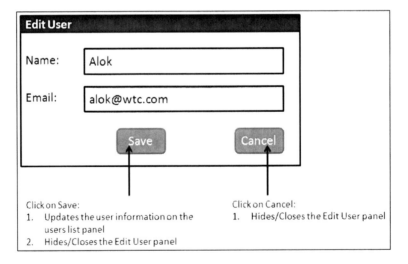

After clicking on **Save**, the modified user's information will appear on the user list.

Application design

Let us delve deeper into the application that we want to create in ExtJS and Touch. First, let us identify the different views we would like to have in our application. Deciding about the number of views is totally based on the granularity at which you would like to work on. For example, in this application we can define the panel's top title bar as one view that can show a **Title** and a **Refresh** button on the top of a panel to which it is added. Similarly, the **Save** and **Cancel** buttons on the **Edit User** panel can be encapsulated inside the **ButtonBar** view and can be used on the panels where we need to show those two buttons. If tomorrow, one more button such as the **Help** button needs to be added to it so that we start seeing three buttons in all the places in the application, then making that change would be a lot faster and cleaner. However, if we take a different level of granularity, then we will have a panel with the title bar showing the panel title and a **Refresh** icon. Also, we would have an **Edit User** panel with the **Save** and **Cancel** buttons. So, is there a rule to decide when I should have the **Save** and **Cancel** buttons added to the panel, directly, and when I should wrap them into a **ButtonBar** view and add it to the panel? Well, there is no pre-defined rule or recommendation from Sencha. It totally depends upon how you want to model your application to achieve the goals, such as re-usability, agility (incorporating changes quickly), maintainability, and testability. So, if you see that the **Save** and **Cancel** buttons would appear in multiple places in your application, then that tells us that it would be better to create a **ButtonBar** view and use it across the panels in the application.

For simplicity, we will be defining the following views:

- **Users List**: This shows the list of users for all or a particular department
- **Departments List**: This shows the list of departments
- **Edit User**: This shows the selected user information and allows the editing of the same

Now, let us list out the models. Going by the same goals, we will define the following models:

- **User**: This model represents a user
- **Department**: This model represents a department

Since we will be showing a list of users and departments, we will define the following stores:

- **Users**: This contains a collection of User models and will be used to show the departments' list
- **Departments**: This contains a collection of Department models and will be used to show the users list

The store would load the data from a data source. So, let us define the following datafiles which we will be using in the application to load the data in the different stores:

- `users.json`

  This datafile contains a list of users. Information, such as `name`, `email`, and the `department` code is returned for a user `id`, which identifies a user uniquely.

  ```
  {
      success: true,
      users: [
          {id: 1, name: 'Sunil',    email: 'sunil@wtc.com',
  department:'FIN'},
          {id: 2, name: 'Sujit', email: 'sujit@wtc.com',
  department:'FIN'},
          {id: 3, name: 'Alok', email: 'alok@wtc.com',
  department:'DEV'},
          {id: 4, name: 'Pradeep', email: 'pradeep@wtc.com',
  department:'SAL'},
          {id: 5, name: 'Ajit', email: 'ajit@wtc.com',
  department:'DEV'}
      ]
  }
  ```

  The `users` field in the JSON contains the users list. For each user, it contains the `id`, `name`, `email`, and `department` code. The `success` property is used to report the application's success/failure, and the `true` property indicates success.

- `departments.json`

  This datafile contains a list of departments with their `code`, `name`, and `location`.

  ```
  {
      success: true,
      departments: [
          {code: 'FIN', name: 'Finance',    location: 'Hyderabad'},
          {code: 'SAL', name: 'Sales', location: 'Hyderabad'},
          {code: 'DEV', name: 'Development', location: 'Agra'}
      ]
  }
  ```

The `departments` field in the JSON contains the department list. For each department, it contains `code`, `name`, and `location`. The `success` property is used to report the application's success/failure, and the `true` property indicates success.

One last thing we are left with is the controller. Again, the question is whether we should have one controller or multiple controllers? I generally recommend having one controller per entity in the application. In our application, we have got two entities – User and Department. So, we will have the following controllers:

- **Users**: This controller is used to manage the views related to the User entity
- **Departments**: This controller is used to manage the views related to the Department entity

Now that we have identified all the pieces of our application, let us see how each one of them needs to be implemented in ExtJS and Touch and understand how they need to be assembled to create a functional application, which meets the requirements that we have outlined earlier.

ExtJS-based application

In ExtJS, we will be dealing with the following classes:

- `Ext.app.Application`: This is the application class
- `Ext.app.Controller`: This class provides the controller functionality
- `Ext.container.Container, Ext.Component`: This class and its sub-classes are used for providing views
- `Ext.data.Model`: This class helps us represent a model which the `Ext.data.Store` class can understand
- `Ext.data.Store`: This class contains a collection of `Ext.data.Model` type objects and is used on the components to show a list of records

Folder structure

In Sencha MVC architecture, folder structure is very important as the underlying class loading uses the pre-defined rules, related to the folder structure, to load the classes automatically for us, on demand. More about the class loading and how it works will be covered in the next chapter.

Create a folder named extjsapp under WebContent in the
SenchaArchitectureBook project, which we created in *Chapter 1, Sencha MVC
Architecture*, and add the following files and directories:

- app: This is the main application directory. This will have the model, view,
  controller, and store directories
    - ○ model
    - ○ User.js
    - ○ Department.js
    - ○ store
    - ○ Users.js
    - ○ Departments.js
    - ○ view
    - ○ user\List.js
    - ○ user\Edit.js
    - ○ department\List.js
    - ○ Viewport.js
    - ○ controller
    - ○ Users.js
    - ○ Departments.js

- data: This contains the JSON datafiles
- extjs-4.1.0-rc1: This contains the ExtJS framework
- app.js: This contains the entry point code for the application
- index.html: This is the HTML for the application

Once created, the folder structure should look like the following screenshot:

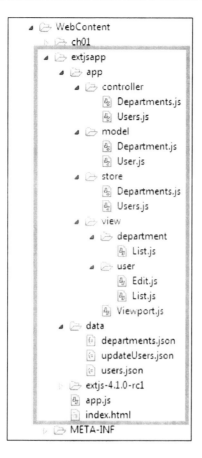

Model

Let us define the different models for our application. We will have the following models:

- User
- Department

User

Save the following code inside the app\model\User.js file:

```
Ext.define('AM.model.User', {
    extend: 'Ext.data.Model',
    fields: ['id', 'name', 'email','department'],
});
```

The code that we just used defines a User model, which represents a user in the application. AM.model in the class name is important as it is used by the loader to identify the file, which contains the class definition and loads the same. AM is the name of the application, which acts as a namespace. This has been explained, in detail, in the later part of this section.

Department

Save the following code inside the app\model\Department.js file:

```
Ext.define('AM.model.Department', {
    extend: 'Ext.data.Model',
    fields: ['code', 'name', 'location']
});
```

The code that we just used defines a Department model, which represents a department in the application.

Store

Similar to the models, now let us define the stores. In the application, we will have the following stores:

- Users
- Departments

Users

Save the following code inside the app\store\Users.js file:

```
Ext.define('AM.store.Users', {
    extend: 'Ext.data.Store',
    model: 'AM.model.User',
    autoLoad: true,  //loads data as soon as the store is initialized

    proxy: {
        type: 'ajax',
        api: {
            read: 'data/users.json'
```

```
        },
        reader: {
            type: 'json',
            root: 'users',
            successProperty: 'success'
        }
    },


    filterUsersByDepartment: function(deptCode) {
      this.clearFilter();
      this.filter([{
            property: 'department',
            value: deptCode
        }]);
    },

    refresh: function() {
      this.clearFilter();
    }
});
```

The code that we just used defines a store, which keeps a collection of `User` models, indicated by the `model` property. The `proxy` property contains the information about the AJAX proxy that the store will use to call the specified read URL `data/user.json` to load the users. `Reader` is configured based on the `users.json` file where the `root` must be set to the config in the `users.json` file, which contains the user records, which is `users`.

The `autoLoad: true` property will tell the framework to load the data into the store as soon as the store is instantiated.

The `filterUsersByDepartment` method is a public method, which filters the store using the specified department code. This method is called as part of the handling of the selection of a specific department from the **Departments List** view.

The `refresh` method is a public method, which clears all the filters applied on the store data and shows all the records in the store. This method is called as part of the handling of the **Refresh** button click on the **Users List** view.

Departments

Save the following code inside the app\store\Departments.js file:

```
Ext.define('AM.store.Departments', {
    extend: 'Ext.data.Store',
    model: 'AM.model.Department',
    autoLoad: true,

    proxy: {
        type: 'ajax',
        api: {
            read: 'data/departments.json'
        },
        reader: {
            type: 'json',
            root: 'departments',
            successProperty: 'success'
        }
    }
});
```

The code that we just used defines store, which would contain the departments data. Every entry in it will be a Department model.

View

The application will have the following views:

- **User List**
- **Edit User**
- **Department List**

User List

Save the following code inside the app\view\user\List.js file:

```
Ext.define('AM.view.user.List' ,{
    extend: 'Ext.grid.Panel',
    alias : 'widget.userlist',

    title : 'All Users',
    store: 'Users',

    columns: [
        {header: 'Name',  dataIndex: 'name',  flex: 1},
```

```
            {header: 'Email', dataIndex: 'email', flex: 1}
        ],

        tools:[{
            type:'refresh',
            tooltip: 'Refresh',
            handler: function(){
              var pnl = this.up('userlist');
              pnl.getStore().refresh();
              pnl.setTitle('All Users');
            }
        }],

        filterUsersByDepartment: function(deptCode) {
            this.getStore().filterUsersByDepartment(deptCode);
        }
    });
```

The code that we just used defines the **User List** view, which extends a grid panel. The `Users` store is associated with it. The grid will show two columns `Name` and `Email`, and has a toolbar with the **Refresh** button. Since, the refresh logic is private to the **User List** view, the handler is registered in the view class where it is refreshes the store and sets the title correctly.

The `filterUsersByDepartment` method is a public method, which filters the store using the specified department code. This method is called as part of the handling of the selection of a specific department from the **Departments List** view. This relies on the store's `filterUsersByDepartment` entity to accomplish the task.

`userlist` has been mentioned as an alias, which can be used as `xtype` for the **User List** view.

User Edit

Save the following code inside the `app\view\user\Edit.js` file:

```
Ext.define('AM.view.user.Edit', {
    extend: 'Ext.window.Window',
    alias : 'widget.useredit',

    requires: ['Ext.form.Panel'],

    title : 'Edit User',
    layout: 'fit',
    autoShow: true,
    height: 120,
```

```
        width: 280,

    initComponent: function() {
        this.items = [
            {
                xtype: 'form',
                padding: '5 5 0 5',
                border: false,
                style: 'background-color: #fff;',

                items: [
                    {
                        xtype: 'textfield',
                        name : 'name',
                        fieldLabel: 'Name'
                    },
                    {
                        xtype: 'textfield',
                        name : 'email',
                        fieldLabel: 'Email'
                    }
                ]
            }
        ];

        this.buttons = [
            {
                text: 'Save',
                action: 'save'
            },
            {
                text: 'Cancel',
                action: 'cancel'
            }
        ];

        this.callParent(arguments);
    }
});
```

The code that we just used defines the **Edit User** view. This extends the `Window`
and has a form panel, which contains two text fields and two buttons.

The `name` property on the text fields has been specified and their value must match with the field name on the `User` model. This will be helpful in loading the data from the model into the form.

`useredit` has been mentioned as an alias, which can be used as `xtype` for the **Edit User** view.

Department List

Save the following code inside the `app\view\department\List.js` file:

```
Ext.define('AM.view.department.List' ,{
    extend: 'Ext.grid.Panel',
    alias : 'widget.departmentlist',

    title : 'Departments',
    store: 'Departments',

    columns: [
        {header: 'Name', dataIndex: 'name', flex: 1},
        {header: 'Location', dataIndex: 'location', flex: 1}
    ]
});
```

In the code we just used, we defined the **Department List** view, which extends a grid panel and uses the `Departments` store. It has two columns, `Name` and `Location`. `departmentlist` has been mentioned as an alias, which can be used as `xtype` for the **Department List** view.

Viewport

Save the following code inside the `app\view\Viewport.js` file:

```
Ext.define('AM.view.Viewport', {
    extend: 'Ext.container.Viewport',

    requires: ['AM.view.department.List', 'AM.view.user.List'],

    layout: 'border',
    config: {
        items: [{
            region: 'west',
            width: 200,
              xtype: 'departmentlist'
        }, {
            region: 'center',
```

```
                xtype: 'userlist'
        }]
    }
});
```

Controller

In the application, we will have the following controllers:

- Users
- Departments

Users

Save the following code inside the app\controller\Users.js file:

```
Ext.define('AM.controller.Users', {
    extend: 'Ext.app.Controller',

    config: {
      stores: ['Users'],

        models: ['User'],

        views: ['user.Edit', 'user.List'],

        refs: [{
            ref: 'usersList',
            selector: 'userlist'
        }]
    },

    init: function(app) {
        this.control({
            'userlist dataview': {
                itemdblclick: this.editUser
            },
            'useredit button[action=save]': {
                click: this.updateUser
            },
            'useredit button[action=cancel]': {
                click: this.cancelEditUser
            }
        });

        app.on('departmentselected', function(app, model) {
```

```
                this.getUsersStore().filterUsersByDepartment(model.
    get('code'));
            this.getUsersList().setTitle(model.get('name') + ' Users');
        }, this);
    },

    editUser: function(grid, record) {
        var edit = Ext.create('AM.view.user.Edit').show();

        edit.down('form').loadRecord(record);
    },

    updateUser: function(button) {
        var win    = button.up('window'),
            form   = win.down('form'),
            record = form.getRecord(),
            values = form.getValues();

        record.set(values);
        win.close();
            },
    cancelEditUser: function(button) {
        var win    = button.up('window');
        win.close();
    }
});
```

In the code that we just used, we defined the Users controller, which manages the userlist and edituser views. It also uses the Users store and the User model. All these are listed in a controller using the views, stores, and models properties.

The init method in a controller class is called by the framework to initialize the controller, even before the application is launched. The typical task that we do here is registering the handlers for the different view elements. This is done by calling the control method of the controller, where we specify the xtype-based selectors to identify the view component (for example, useredit button[action=save] identifies the **Save** button on the **Edit User** window) and register their event handlers.

The controller also handles the departmentselected event in the application, which is fired by the Departments controller when a particular department is selected. Let us see what the Departments controller looks like.

Departments

Save the following code inside the app\controller\Departments.js file:

```
Ext.define('AM.controller.Departments', {
    extend: 'Ext.app.Controller',

    config: {
      stores: ['Departments'],

        models: ['Department'],

        views: ['department.List']
    },

    init: function() {
        this.control({
            'departmentlist': {
                itemclick: this.showDepartmentUser
            }
        });
    },

    showDepartmentUser: function(grid, model, itemEl, idx, e, eOpts) {
      var app = this.application;
        app.fireEvent('departmentselected', app, model);
    }
});
```

The code that we just used defines the Departments controller, which manages the department-related view, model, and the store. It fires the departmentselected event on the application when a department is selected.

Application

Save the following code inside the app.js file:

```
Ext.application({
    name: 'AM',   //application name that becomes the namespace

    // automatically create an instance of AM.view.Viewport
    autoCreateViewport: true,

    controllers: [
        'Users', 'Departments'
    ]
});
```

In the code that we just used, we are initializing the application. The `name: 'AM'` property is a very important property. It creates an automatic namespace for our application. Due to this, we defined all the classes starting with `AM`, for example, `AM.model.User`. Once specified, if the framework comes across with any class name starting with `AM`, it will look for that class in the app folder. For example, when it encounters `AM.model.User`, it will look for the `User.js` file inside the `app\model` folder. Similarly, for `AM.view.user.List` it will look for the `List.js` file inside the `app\view\user` folder.

The `autoCreateViewport:true` property will tell the framework to automatically look for the `Viewport.js` file inside the `app\view` folder and create the viewport using it.

An application is a collection of controllers, which internally manage one or more views to accomplish the overall requirement. All the controllers, which constitute the application, need to be specified as part of the `controllers` property. A fully qualified name, such as `AM.controller.Users`, is not required as the framework will automatically look for the `Users` controller inside the `app\controller` folder.

index.html

Save the following code inside the `index.html` file:

```
<html>
<head>
    <meta http-equiv="Content-Type" content="text/html;
charset=utf-8">
    <title id="page-title">Account Manager</title>

    <link rel="stylesheet" type="text/css" href="extjs-4.1.0-rc1/
resources/css/ext-all.css">
    <script type="text/javascript" src="extjs-4.1.0-rc1/ext-debug.
js"></script>

    <script type="text/javascript" src="app.js"></script>
</head>
<body>

</body>
</html>
```

Publish the application to Apache Tomcat, **Start** the server, and access
`http://<host>:<port>/SenchaArchitectureBook/extjsapp/index.html`
in the browser. You shall see the following screen:

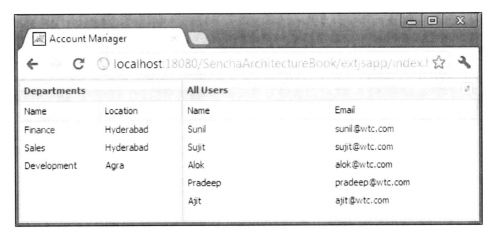

Selecting a particular department from the **Departments** list shows the users from
the selected department, as shown in the following screenshot:

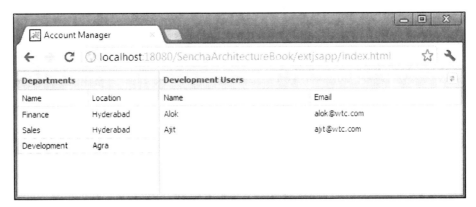

Double-click on the user record. This will bring up the **Edit User** view with the
values populated from the selected user, as shown in the following screenshot:

Make some change to the user information, say, **Name**, and click on **Save**. We shall see the updated information in the users list, as shown in the following screenshot:

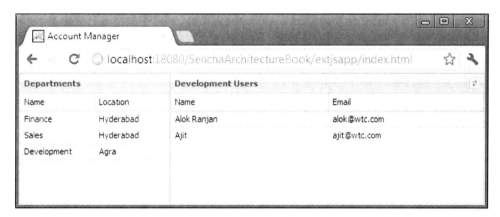

Click on the **Refresh** icon on the users list. This will reload all the users in the users list.

Sencha Touch-based application

For the MVC architecture, as ExtJS and Touch have a lot of things in common, the overall approach would remain similar for Touch as well. In Sencha Touch, we will be dealing with the following classes:

- `Ext.app.Application`: This is the application class
- `Ext.app.Controller`: This class provides the controller functionality
- `Ext.Container`, `Ext.Component`: These classes and their sub-classes are used for providing views

- `Ext.data.Model`: This class helps us represent a model which the `Ext.data.Store` class can understand
- `Ext.data.Store`: This class contains a collection of `Ext.data.Model` type objects and is used on the components to show a list of records

Folder structure

Create a folder `touchapp` under `WebContent` in the `SenchaArchitectureBook` project, which we created in *Chapter 1, Sencha MVC Architecture*, and add the following files and directories:

- app: This is the main application directory. It will have a model, view, controller, and store directories:
  - model
  - User.js
  - Department.js
  - store
  - Users.js
  - Departments.js
  - view
  - user\List.js
  - user\Edit.js
  - department\List.js
  - controller
  - Users.js
  - Departments.js

- data: This contains the JSON datafiles.
- sencha-touch-2.0.0: This contains the ExtJS framework.
- app.js: This contains the entry point code for the application.
- index.html: This is the HTML for the application.

Once created, the folder structure should look like the following screenshot:

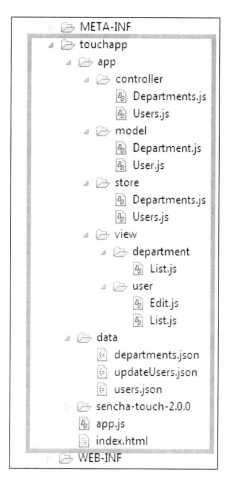

Model

We will have the following models:

- User
- Department

User

Save the following code inside the app\model\User.js file:

```
Ext.define('AM.model.User', {
    extend: 'Ext.data.Model',
    config: {
        fields: ['id', 'name', 'email', 'department']
    }
});
```

The code that we just used defines the User model.

Department

Save the following code inside the app\model\Department.js file:

```
Ext.define('AM.model.Department', {
    extend: 'Ext.data.Model',
    config: {
        fields: ['code', 'name', 'location']
    }
});
```

The code that we just used defines the Department model.

Store

In the application we will have the following stores:

- Users
- Departments

Users

Save the following code inside the app\store\Users.js file:

```
Ext.define('AM.store.Users', {
    extend: 'Ext.data.Store',

    config: {
        autoLoad: true,
        model: 'AM.model.User',
        storeId: 'Users',
        proxy: {
            type: 'ajax',
            api: {
                read: 'data/users.json'
```

```
            },
            reader: {
                type: 'json',
                rootProperty: 'users'
            }
        }

    },

    filterUsersByDepartment: function(deptCode) {
      this.clearFilter();
      this.filter([{
            property: 'department',
            value: deptCode
        }]);
    },

    refresh: function() {
      this.clearFilter();
    }
});
```

The code that we just used defines the Users store, which contains the collection of User models.

Departments

Save the following code inside the app\store\Departments.js file:

```
Ext.define('AM.store.Departments', {
    extend: 'Ext.data.Store',
    model: 'AM.model.Department',

    config: {
        autoLoad: true,
        model: 'AM.model.Department',
        storeId: 'Departments',
        proxy: {
            type: 'ajax',
            api: {
                read: 'data/departments.json'
            },
            reader: {
                type: 'json',
                rootProperty: 'departments'
```

```
            }
          }
        }
      }
    });
```

The code that we just used defines the `Departments` store, which contains the collection of `Department` models.

View

The application will have the following views:

* **User List**
* **Edit User**
* **Department List**

User List

Save the following code inside the `app\view\user\List.js` file:

```
Ext.define('AM.view.user.List' ,{
    extend: 'Ext.Container',
    alias : 'widget.userlist',

    config: {
        ui: 'light',
        layout: {
            type: 'fit'
        },
        items: [
            {
                xtype: 'toolbar',
                docked: 'top',
                title: 'All Users',
                defaults: {
                    iconMask: true
                },
                items: [{
                    xtype: 'spacer'
                },
                {
                    iconCls: 'refresh',
                    ui: 'confirm',
                    handler: function(){
                        this.up('userlist').down('list').getStore().
```

```
refresh();
                          this.up('toolbar').setTitle('All Users');
                    }
               }]
          },
          {
               xtype: 'list',
               height: '100%',
               ui: 'round',
               itemTpl: [
                                '<div style="float:left;">{name}</div>',
                                '<div style="float:left;position:absolut
e;padding-left:150px;">{email}</div>'
               ],
               store: 'Users',
               onItemDisclosure: true
          }
     ]
   }
});
```

The code that we just used defines the **User List** view by extending the `Container` class. It shows a list of users with the disclosure option (refer to the Sencha Touch API documentation of `Ext.dataview.List` for more detail) and a toolbar on the top with the **Title** and the **Refresh** button. The list uses the `Users` store to load data. Similar to the ExtJS-based app, the handler for the **Refresh** button is implemented inside the view as the logic is local to the view.

The `userlist` alias will act as `xtype` for this view.

User Edit

Save the following code inside the `app\view\user\Edit.js` file:

```
Ext.define('AM.view.user.Edit', {
    extend: 'Ext.form.Panel',
    alias : 'widget.useredit',

    config: {
        ui: 'light',
        items: [
            {
                xtype: 'titlebar',
                docked: 'top',
                title: 'Edit User'
            },
```

```
        {
            xtype: 'textfield',
            label: 'Name',
            name: 'name',
            labelWidth: '50%',
            required: true
        },
        {
            xtype: 'textfield',
            label: 'Email',
            name: 'email',
            labelWidth: '50%',
            required: true
        },
        {
            xtype: 'toolbar',
            docked: 'bottom',
            items: [{
                xtype: 'button',
                margin: 10,
                align: 'left',
                ui: 'confirm',
                action: 'save',
                text: 'Save'
            }, {
                xtype: 'spacer'
            }, {
            xtype: 'button',
                margin: 10,
                align: 'right',
                ui: 'decline',
                action: 'cancel',
                text: 'Cancel'

            }]
        }

        ]
    }
});
```

The code that we just used defines the **Edit User** view by extending the form panel. It contains two text fields and a bottom toolbar with **Save** and **Cancel** buttons.

The useredit alias will be used as xtype for this view.

Department List

Save the following code inside the `app\view\department\List.js` file:

```
Ext.define('AM.view.department.List' ,{
    extend: 'Ext.Container',
    alias : 'widget.departmentlist',

    config: {
        ui: 'light',
        layout: {
            type: 'fit'
        },
        items: [
            {
                xtype: 'titlebar',
                docked: 'top',
                title: 'Departments'
            },
            {
                xtype: 'list',
                height: '100%',
                ui: 'round',
                itemTpl: [
        '<div style="float:left;">{name}</div>',
        '<div style="float:left;position:absolute;padding-
left:150px;">{location}</div>'
                ],
                store: 'Departments',
                onItemDisclosure: false
            }
        ]
    }
});
```

The code that we just used defines the **Department List** view by extending the `Container` class. It shows a list of departments without the disclosure option. The list uses the `Departments` store to load data.

The `departmentlist` alias will act as the `xtype` for this view.

Controller

In the application, we will have the following controllers:

- Users
- Departments

Users

Save the following code inside the `app\controller\Users.js` file:

```
Ext.define('AM.controller.Users', {
    extend: 'Ext.app.Controller',

    config: {
        stores: ['Users'],

        models: ['User'],

        views: ['user.Edit', 'user.List'],

        refs: {
            usersPanel: 'userlist'
        }
    },
    init: function(app) {
        this.control({
            'userlist list': {
                disclose: this.editUser
            },
            'useredit button[action=save]': {
                tap: this.updateUser
            },
            'useredit button[action=cancel]': {
                tap: this.cancelEditUser
            }
        });

        app.on('departmentselected', function(app, model) {
            this.getUsersStore().filterUsersByDepartment(model.
get('code'));
            this.getUsersPanel().down('toolbar').setTitle(model.
get('name') + ' Users');
        }, this);
    },
    editUser: function(view, model, t, index, e, eOpts) {
```

```
            var edit = Ext.create('AM.view.user.Edit');
            Ext.Viewport.add(edit);

            edit.setRecord(model);
            Ext.Viewport.setActiveItem(edit);
        },
        updateUser: function(button, e ,eOpts) {
            var form   = button.up('formpanel');
            var record = form.getRecord(),
                values = form.getValues();

            record.set(values);
            this.getUsersStore().sync();
            Ext.Viewport.setActiveItem(0);
        },
        cancelEditUser: function(button, e ,eOpts) {
            Ext.Viewport.setActiveItem(0);
        },
        showUsersList: function() {
            var list = Ext.create('AM.view.user.List');
            Ext.Viewport.add(list);
        },
        getUsersStore: function() {
            return this.getUsersPanel().down('list').getStore();
        }
    });
```

The code that we just used defines the `Users` controller.

Departments

Save the following code inside the `app\controller\Departments.js` file:

```
Ext.define('AM.controller.Departments', {
    extend: 'Ext.app.Controller',

    config: {
        stores: ['Departments'],

        models: ['Department'],

        views: ['department.List']
    },

    init: function() {
```

```
            this.control({
                'departmentlist list': {
                    itemtap: this.showDepartmentUser
                }
            });
        },

        showDepartmentUser: function(view, idx, t, model, e, eOpts) {
            var app = this.initialConfig.application;
            app.fireEvent('departmentselected', app, model);
        }
    });
```

The code that we just used defines the `Departments` controller.

Application

Save the following code inside the `app.js` file:

```
Ext.application({
    name: 'AM',

    // dependencies
    controllers: ['Users', 'Departments'],

    // launch application
    launch: function() {
        var config = {
          layout: 'fit',
          items: [{
            xtype: 'departmentlist',
            docked: 'left',
            width: 400
          }, {
            xtype: 'userlist'
          }]

        };

        Ext.Viewport.add(config);
    }
});
```

In the last line, we added the panel, with `department list` and `user list`, to the viewport. Since the viewport concept is not very straightforward on touch devices, the framework wraps those differences and provides us with static methods, such as add, to add content to it.

index.html

Save the following code inside the `index.html` file:

```
<!DOCTYPE html PUBLIC "-//W3C//DTD HTML 4.01 Transitional//EN"
"http://www.w3.org/TR/html4/loose.dtd">
<html>
<head>
<meta http-equiv="Content-Type" content="text/html;
charset=ISO-8859-1">
<title>Account Manager</title>

<!-- Sencha Touch specific files -->
<link rel="stylesheet" type="text/css" href="sencha-touch-2.0.0/
resources/css/sencha-touch.css">
<script type="text/javascript" src="sencha-touch-2.0.0/sencha-touch-
all-debug.js"></script>

<!-- Application specific files -->
<script type="text/javascript" src="app.js"></script>

</head>
<body>

</body>
</html>
```

Publish the application to Apache Tomcat, **Start** the server, and access
`http://<host>:<port>/SenchaArchitectureBook/touchapp/index.html` in the
Webkit browser. You should see the following screen:

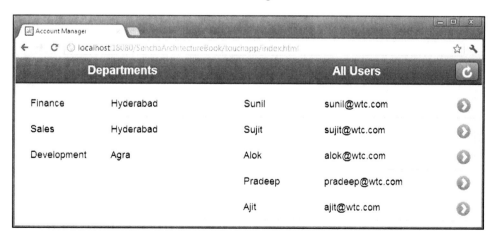

Selecting a particular department from the **Departments** list shows the users from the selected department, as shown in the following screenshot:

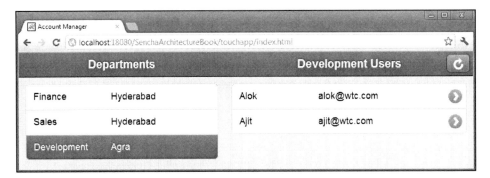

Double-click on the **User Record** button. This will bring up the **Edit User** view with the values populated from the selected user, as shown in the following screenshot:

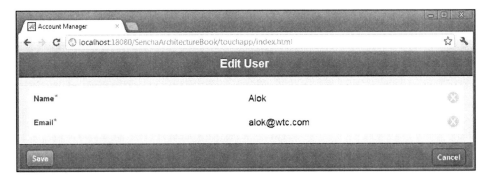

Make some change to the user information, say, **Name**, and click on **Save**. We should see the updated information in the users list, as shown in the following screenshot:

Click on the **Refresh** icon on the users list. This will reload all the users in the users list.

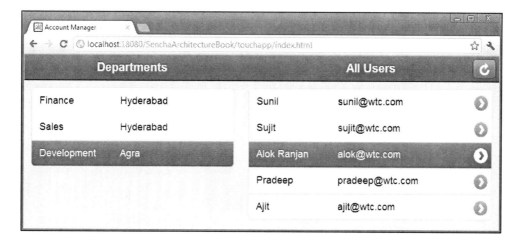

Summary

In this chapter we took a sample application and learned how to model it as per the MVC architecture and map the different building blocks to the classes provided by ExtJS and Sencha Touch. The application involved how to identify the views, models, and controllers in an application, how to make use of multiple controllers within an application and pass the data and the control between them to achieve the overall application behavior. We also looked at some of the rules related to class naming conventions, folder structure, and so on, which is required to get the application up and running.

In the subsequent chapters, we will look into each of the building blocks in detail, and also look at the underlying framework infrastructure which acts as the foundation for the MVC architecture.

3
Building Blocks

In the previous chapter, we built an MVC architecture-based application from scratch. We looked at the different classes the Ext JS and Sencha Touch frameworks offer, which helped us model our application as per the MVC architecture.

In Ext JS, the following classes constitute the implementation of an MVC architecture:

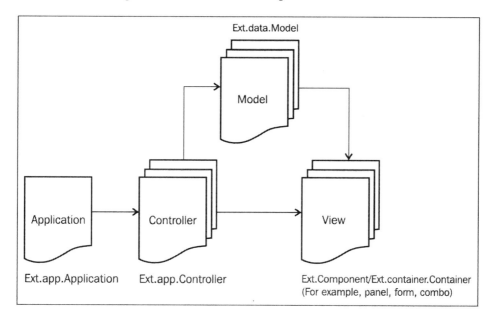

However, in Sencha Touch, the following classes constitute the implementation of an MVC architecture:

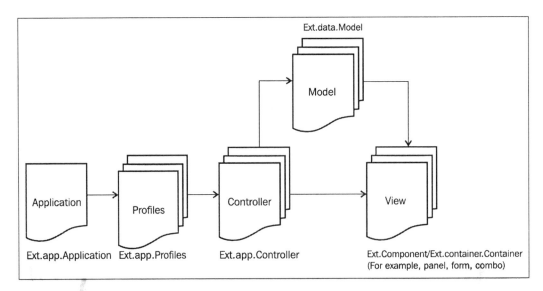

In this chapter, we will look into the detail of each of these classes, which act as the building blocks for creating applications. We will look at the function of each class and the behaviors they support.

Model

Model represents a state of the application and helps share the state across various views in an application. It typically contains the fields to store data/state and knows how to persist itself through the data package. In the previous chapters, we defined two models—Department and User. Each one of them had fields which represented the entity, either Department or User.

The model related code is kind of common across Ext JS and Touch frameworks. Their internal implementations differ on each of these frameworks. However, the interface remains consistent. We will highlight the differences wherever applicable.

In the estjsapp applications, we defined the following models:

```
Ext.define('AM.model.Department', {
    extend: 'Ext.data.Model',
    fields: ['code', 'name', 'location']
});

Ext.define('AM.model.User', {
```

```
    extend: 'Ext.data.Model',
    fields: ['id', 'name', 'email', 'department']
});
```

In the `touchapp` applications, we defined the following models:

```
Ext.define('AM.model.Department', {
    extend: 'Ext.data.Model',
    config: {
        fields: ['code', 'name', 'location']
    }
});

Ext.define('AM.model.User', {
    extend: 'Ext.data.Model',
    config: {
        fields: ['id', 'name', 'email', 'department']
    }
});
```

Apart from the usage of `config` in Touch, the definitions are pretty much the same.

Every model must extend `Ext.data.Model` and must at least have the `fields` defined. A model class offers the following:

- Has `fields`, which allows us to list out the attributes of an entity, for example, `e-mail` of an `user`.
- Can apply validations on the field values. There are built-in validations—`presence`, `length`, `inclusion`, `exclusion`, and `format`. And, if needed, we can also define additional validation types and use them to validate the data inside a model; for example, `presence` can help us to validate if name is present on the model or not. For this, the model has got a validations config property where we list out the different validations that we would like to apply on the model instance. After the validations are configured, the `validate()` method on a model instance must be called to validate that instance using the specified `validations` list. More details about it are available on the documentation of the `Ext.data.Model` class. *Chapter 5, Dealing with Data and Data Sources* of *Sencha Touch Cookbook, Packt Publishing,* also discusses this in detail and provides additional recipes to define a custom validation.

- Can establish associations with other models. In our example, we had two models and two JSON files, each providing the data about a specific entity. In case your JSON file contains the department and their users in a single file, then it is possible to establish associations between the `Department` and the `User` model so that in a single load of the JSON file, both the `Department` and their `User` models are created and are ready for use. There are two types of associations the framework supports — `hasMany` (one-to-many) and `belongsTo` (many-to-one). So, we may say a `Department` has many `User` models and that a `User` belongs to a `Department`. More detail about it is available in the documentation of the `Ext.data.Model` class.

- Can set up a `proxy` to connect to a data source. A proxy is a way to connect to a data source and operate on that to create, read, update, and destroy. In our example, we did not configure the proxy on the model. Rather, we configured it on the store. However, if needed, a proxy can also be specified on a model.

The following operations can be performed on a model instance:

- `load`: This loads a model from a data source using the `proxy` configuration.

- `save`: This saves a model to a data source using the `proxy` configuration. If the `id` field is empty, the `create` request is sent to the data source. Otherwise, the `update` request is sent.

- `erase`: This destroys a model using the configured proxy. This does not destroy the model instance on the client side. After the data source returns success, it notifies the store, which it is joined to, and the store takes care of removing that model instance from the client side.

- `reject`: This is used by the store usually to revert the changes made to the model instance during the editing, for example, the e-mail ID is changed as part of the user edit.

- `commit`: This commits the changes to the mode instance since either the creation or the last commit operation. This does not send the data to the data source.

- `validate`: This validates the model instance against all the configured validations. This returns an array of errors containing the field and the message for all the fields that did not pass the validation.

- `destroy`: This destroys the model instance from the client side. To destroy a model instance from the data source, one must use the `erase` operation, as discussed previously.

- `copy`: This helps us create a copy of an existing model instance. The ID of the new model can either be specified while calling this method or the framework will automatically generate it.

A model can very well participate in the editing operation and can help us keep track of the changes. The following operations can be performed on a model instance as part of editing:

- `beginEdit`: This marks the beginning of the editing of the model. This can, loosely, be compared with transaction start.

- `endEdit`: This marks the end of the editing. It can, loosely, be compared with transaction end.

- `cancelEdit`: This allows us to cancel any edits made to the model instance after `beginEdit`. This can, loosely, be compared with transaction rollback.

- `changedWhileEditing`: This helps us to check if the underlying model instance has changed during an edit.

- `getChanges`: This helps us to get the list of fields whose values have changed during the edit operation. In Ext JS framework, the method name is `getModifiedFieldNames`.

- `isModified`: This helps us to check if a particular field value has changed in the model instance.

The operations mentioned previously notify the stores, based on which the store updates itself and notifies the view of the change.

Store

Store contains a collection of models and can be specified on various components to help them present the data in their own unique way.

In the `estjsapp` applications, this is how we defined a store:

```
Ext.define('AM.store.Departments', {
    extend: 'Ext.data.Store',
    model: 'AM.model.Department',
    autoLoad: true,

    proxy: {
        type: 'ajax',
        api: {
            read: 'data/departments.json'
        },
        reader: {
            type: 'json',
            root: 'departments',
            successProperty: 'success'
        }
```

```
        }
    });
```

In the `touchapp` applications, this is how we defined a store:

```
Ext.define('AM.store.Departments', {
    extend: 'Ext.data.Store',
    alias: 'store.Departments',

    config: {
        autoLoad: true,
        model: 'AM.model.Department',
        storeId: 'Departments',
        proxy: {
            type: 'ajax',
            api: {
                read: 'data/departments.json'
            },
            reader: {
                type: 'json',
                rootProperty: 'departments'
            }
        }
    }
});
```

Again, besides the `config` usage in the Touch, the two definitions are the same. Every store must be an instance of `Ext.data.Store` and can contain the models that are of the type, `Ext.data.Model`.

A store class offers the following:

- It has `fields`, which allows us to list out the attributes of an entity, for example, the e-mail of an user.

- It can set up a proxy to connect to a data source. Proxy is a way to connect to a data source and operate on that to create, read, update, and destroy. In our `store` definition, we specified `ajax` as the kind of proxy that we would be using. This selection is based on the kind of data source that we are dealing with. `read` is the URL used by the proxy to read data. The `reader` instance converts the data read from the data source to a model instance. Similar to read, we can specify URLs for other CRUD operations that the proxy supports.

- `autoLoad`: This allows us to indicate whether the data shall be loaded immediately after the store is initialized by the framework or an explicit `load` method will be called to initiate the loading. `true` indicates automatic loading.

- `autoSync`: This allows us to indicate whether the modifications to the store models shall be synched up automatically, or if an explicit `sync` call will be called. Value `true` indicates automatic sync.

- Sorting: Sorting can be carried out on the data. This sorting can either be done on the client side or on the server side.

- Grouping: Data can be grouped either on the client side or on the server side.

- Filtering: Data can be filtered either on the client side, or if on the server side.

- A model must be specified on a store. Reader uses this information to convert the incoming data from the data source to the specified model.

- Scrolling buffer (pre-fetch page) is supported on the Ext JS version of the store.

Following operations can be performed on a `store` instance:

- `load`: This loads data from the data source using the specified `proxy`. If `autoLoad` is specified as `false`, this method needs to be called to get the store loaded.

- `sync`: This syncs up the changes made to the store data.

For any change to the data collection, the store notifies the view, which is associated with it so that the views can show the updated data.

View

Every view is a component in Ext JS as well as Touch. The kinds of views (visual presentation) that are available in Ext JS and the kind of behaviors they offer, differ considerably from Touch for the simple reason that each one of them addresses a different segment of devices and those devices have their own uniqueness. The component implementation is very different in the two frameworks. However, at a higher level, both frameworks have got three phases for every view component, shown as follows:

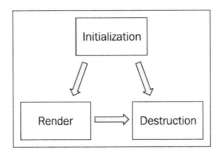

In the Initialization phase, do the following tasks:

1. Register events.
2. Apply styles.
3. Call the hook method of the component/view class, which does the view-specific initialization. For example, `initialize` in Touch and `initComponent` in Ext JS.
4. Register the component to the component manager.
5. Initialize state.
6. Initialize the plugins, if any.
7. Enter the Render phase.

In the Render phase, do the following tasks:

1. Generate elements and add them to the DOM.
2. Apply custom styles.
3. Initialize events.
4. Initialize state information.

In the Destruction phase, do the following tasks:

1. Remove the component from its container.
2. Destroy plugins, if any.
3. Unregister a component from the component manager.
4. Destroy state information.
5. Remove event listeners.
6. Remove elements.

Controller

Controllers act as a central place to handle the events originating from various views. It helps us to take care of the cross-view interactions to build the application flow.

ExtJS

In the Ext JS framework, a controller does the following:

- Uses `Ext.util.Observable` mixin which acts as the foundation for raising events and registering handlers for the events.
- Loads the models, views, stores, and other dependencies mentioned in the requirements, before creation.
- Calls the constructor.
- Creates getter methods for: `model`, `store`, and `view`.
- Creates getter methods for the `ref` objects.
- Creates the components referred in the `ref` config, if references are to be cached (default behavior, unless `forceCreate` is set to `true`). If the component is not cached and `autoCreate` is set to `true` on the `ref` object, then the component is created and added to the cache.

Sencha Touch

In the Touch framework, a controller does the following:

- Uses the `Ext.util.Observable` mixin.
- Creates getter methods for `ref` objects.
- Creates the components referred in the `ref` config. If the component is not cached and `autoCreate` is set to `true` on the `ref` object, then the component is created and added to the cache.

The previous list highlights the differences in the controller implementation on two frameworks. Though the effort is on to implement a consistent interface and behavior across the two frameworks, there are still differences that need to be addressed.

Profile

Profile is applicable only to Sencha Touch and it helps us to build the application which can work on multiple devices. A profile must be created for every device where we handle the device specific layouts and behaviors.

Every profile must extend the `Ext.app.Profile` class and must implement the `isActive` method. During the application's initialization, the framework goes through all the profiles mentioned in the `profiles` config on the `Ext.application` class and executes their `isActive` method, one-by-one. The first profile for which the `isActive` method returns `true` is considered as an active profile. A profile-specific controller, model, view, and store needs to be set on the profile class using the `controllers`, `models`, `views`, and `stores` properties. Let us see what changes we will have to make to our `touchapp` to support profiles.

Say, we are going to support two profiles—`Desktop` and `Phone`. All the behavior that we built in the previous chapter needs to be there for the `Desktop` profile. For `Phone`, we would have a different layout. The following are the steps that we would have to go through to make use of a profile:

1. Create a `profile` folder under the `app` folder.

2. Define a `Desktop` profile class and save the following code inside the `Desktop.js` file inside the `profile` folder:

```
Ext.define('AM.profile.Desktop', {
    extend: 'Ext.app.Profile',

    config: {
      controllers: ['Users', 'Departments'],
      views: ['user.List', 'department.List'],
      stores: ['AM.store.Users', 'AM.store.Departments'],
      models: ['AM.model.User', 'AM.model.Department']
    },

    isActive: function() {
        return Ext.os.is.Desktop;
    },
    launch: function() {
        var config = {
        layout: 'fit',
         items: [{
```

```
        xtype: 'departmentlist',
        docked: 'left',
        width: 400
      }, {
        xtype: 'userlist'
      }]

    };

    Ext.Viewport.add(config);
  }
});
```

Note that we have implemented the isActive method, which returns true if the detected device is the desktop. Additionally, we have implemented the launch method, which contains the code that was inside the app.js file. This way, the layout that we would create would apply to the desktop only.

3. Define another profile for Phone and keep the following code inside Phone. js in the profile folder:

```
Ext.define('AM.profile.Phone', {
    extend: 'Ext.app.Profile',

    isActive: function() {
        return false;                //We do not support Phone...so
always return false
    }
});
```

Since we do not have much to support on the phone, we are returning false from the isActive method.

4. Replace the content of app.js with the following code:

```
Ext.application({
  name: 'AM',
  profiles: ['Desktop', 'Phone']
});
```

Note that we have removed the `launch` method's implementation from the application and moved it to the `launch` method of the `Desktop` profile. We have listed out the two profiles.

5. Create a `desktop` folder under the `controller` and `view` folders and move the controller JS files from `app\controller` to `app\controller\desktop` and from the `app\view` to the `app\view\desktop` folders.

6. Change the class names of the controllers and views to include `desktop` in their names. For example, `AM.controller.Users` will change to `AM.controller.desktop.Users`.

After making all the changes, the folder structure should look as follows:

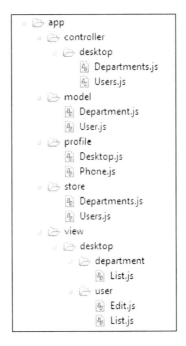

Run the application on your desktop browser and you will see the same output that we saw in the previous chapter. If the application is run on a phone, no view is rendered.

Application

Application glues models, views, controllers, and stores to assemble a complete functional application.

Ext JS

In Ext JS, the `Ext.app.Application` class does the following:

- Extends `Ext.app.Controller`.

- Sets the path on the loader. This helps us in loading the application classes from folders other than the `app` folder.

- Loads the `Viewport` class if `autoCreateViewport` is `true`. When set to `true`, the application will load the `Viewport.js` file from the `app\view` folder.

- Registers the `onReady` method where it instantiates and calls the `init` method on all the controllers.

- Enables `QuickTips` if `enableQuickTips` was set to `true`.

- Creates the `Viewport` if `autoCreateViewport` is `true`.

- Calls the `launch` method of the application.

- Fires the `launch` event.

- Calls the `onLaunch` method of each of the controllers.

Sencha Touch

In Touch, the `Ext.app.Application` class does the following:

- Extends the `Ext.app.Controller` class

- Enables loader so that the dependencies can be loaded

- Loads the profiles, if any

- Instantiates controllers and loads their dependencies

- Instantiates stores

- Identifies the active profile and if there is an active profile, sets the current profile with it

- Loads the dependencies of all the profiles configured for the profile

- Calls the `init` method on all the controllers

- Calls the `launch` method of the active profile

- Calls the `launch` method of the application

- Calls the `launch` method of all the controllers

- Redirects the user to the appropriate controller method call based on the configured routes

Routing and history

In Sencha Touch, controllers can now directly specify which routes they are interested in. This enables us to provide history support within our app, as well as the ability to deeply link to any part of the application that we provide a route for.

This is achieved by setting the `routes` configuration on the controller, shown as follows:

```
refs: {
        usersPanel: 'userlist'
},
routes: {
        'list': 'showUsersList',
        'users/:id': 'showUsersByDepartment'
}
```

In the previous code, we have defined the `routes` config on our `Users` controller where we have defined two routes—`list` and `users/:id`. Each of these two routes corresponds to a method inside the controller. The `list` route points to the `showUsersList` method of the controller and the `users/:id` route points to the `showUsersByDepartment` method. The following is the implementation of the two methods:

```
showUsersList: function() {
    var list = Ext.create('AM.view.user.List');
    Ext.Viewport.add(list);
    Ext.Viewport.setActiveItem(list);
},
showUsersByDepartment: function(deptId) {
    var list = Ext.create('AM.view.user.List');
    Ext.Viewport.add(list);
    Ext.Viewport.setActiveItem(list);

    this.getUsersStore().filterUsersByDepartment(deptId);
}
```

In the `showUsersList` method, we show the list of all the users. In the `showUsersByDepartment` method, we show the list of users filtered based on the department code passed to the method. Once these routes are set up, we can access them by accessing the following URLs:

- http://<host>:<port>/SenchaArchitectureBook/touchapp/#list
- http://<host>:<port>/SenchaArchitectureBook/touchapp/#users/FIN

`FIN` is the code for the Finance department.

Dependency management with loader

If you have noticed, we did not include any JS files (other than `app.js`) in the `index.html` folder and the rest of the files were automatically loaded for us. Well, it is not really automatic. We did indicate the dependencies which the class loader used to load the classes before they are used. We used the `requires`, `controller`, `views`, `models`, and `stores` properties to list out the dependencies. Also, we specified the name for the application which acts as the namespace and tells the loader to load all the classes, with that namespace, from the `app` folder. For example, `AM.view.user.List` will be loaded from the `app/view/user` folder.

In the next chapter, we will look at how the class loader works. However, one thing that we need to understand here is how we load the classes of a different namespace from a different folder. In an enterprise application, this may be a common requirement. For example, let us say there is a `Converter` utility class which is developed and maintained by the middleware team and they use the `MW` namespace for all their classes. The following is the code inside the `Converter.js` file:

```
Ext.define('MW.utils.Converter', {

  convertDeptCodeToName: function(deptCode) {
    if (deptCode === 'FIN')
      return 'Finance';
    if (deptCode === 'DEV')
      return 'Development';
    if (deptCode === 'SAL')
      return 'Sales';
  }

});
```

The `Ext.define` class contains a single method—`convertDeptCodeToName`—which returns the name of the department for the specified department code.

Now, say, the middleware code is kept in the **mw** folder, as shown in the following screenshot:

To make sure that the middleware classes will be loaded, add the following lines of code to **app.js** before the `Ext.application` call:

```
Ext.Loader.setPath({

    'MW': 'mw'
});
```

In the previous code, we have specified the namespace and its folder. Loader uses this path information to load the class with the listed namespace from the configured folder. So, for classes starting with MW, the loader will look for them inside the mw folder.

Now, if any part of the application wants to make use of the `converter` class, then the following lines of code demonstrate how to do that:

```
var mwUtils = Ext.create('MW.utils.Converter', {});
alert(mwUtils.convertDeptCodeToName('FIN'));
```

Summary

In this chapter, we looked at the different classes which are part of the MVC architecture in Ext JS as well as Sencha Touch. We also looked at the function of each of these classes and saw the differences in their behavior and usage. In addition to the common classes—application, controller, model, view (component)—we also looked at the Touch-specific way to handle profiles to encapsulate device-specific behaviors and layout in the applications. Also, we saw how to set up the routes in a Touch application and have the history tracking in place. In the next chapter, we will go further inside the class system, which provides `Ext.define` and `Ext.create` kinds of APIs and understand what the other offerings are, and how to make use of them to build a large enterprise application.

4
Class System

In the previous chapter, we looked into Sencha MVC architecture and implemented a small application where we defined and used various classes. A couple of things we did were as follows:

- We defined classes using `Ext.define`
- We defined classes by extending existing classes
- We instantiated classes using `Ext.create`
- We used aliases while defining the view classes and used them as `xtype`
- We used `ext-debug.js`/`ext.js` for the ExtJS application, and `sencha-touch-debug.js`/`sencha-touch.js` for the Sencha Touch application rather than the xxx-all-xxx variants
- We included only the main `app.js` file in `index.html`

Questions that arose out of these items were:

- Why `Ext.define` and not `Ext.extend`?
- Why `Ext.create` and not the `new` operator?
- How does framework load all my classes, correctly?
- How can the framework use the alias names to identify and instantiate classes?

The two important features, which help the framework to answer the earlier questions, are:

- **Class System**: This feature lays the foundation for defining classes in ExtJS and Sencha Touch
- **Loader**: This feature takes care of resolving the class dependencies by ensuring that the dependencies are loaded before the class can be initialized

In this chapter, we will visit the class system and the loader to understand what they offer and what do they require to provide their functionality.

Class system

Let us look closer at the API doc of `Ext.form.Panel` in ExtJS and Sencha Touch. The following diagram depicts the class hierarchy and some of the dependent classes:

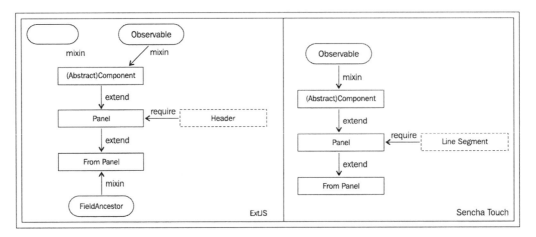

In ExtJS, `Form Panel` extends the `Panel` class and uses the `FieldAncestor` mixin. The `Panel` class extends the `AbstractComponent` class and requires the `Header` class. The `AbstractComponent` class uses `Stateful` and `Observable` as its two mixins to make the component stateful and allows them to fire and handle events.

In Sencha Touch, `Form Panel` extends the `Panel` class. The `Panel` class extends the `AbstractComponent` class and requires the `LineSegment` class. The `AbstractComponent` class uses the `Observable` class as one of its mixins to allow the component to fire and handle events.

Let us take an example and look at what happens when we use the classes as per the class system (for example, use `Ext.create`) and let the loader take care of the dependency loading. Say, we want to create the following UI in ExtJS and Sencha Touch:

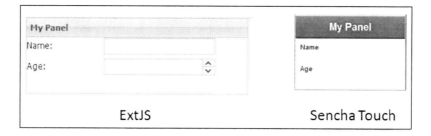

To create the UI, we use the following steps:

1. Create a folder named ch03 under the WebContent folder.

2. Create two folders under ch03 and name them extjs and touch.

3. Create a file named ch03_01.js under the ch03\extjs folder and save the following code inside it:

```
Ext.onReady(function() {

    var pnl = Ext.create('Ext.panel.Panel', {
        title: 'My Panel',
        renderTo: Ext.getBody(),
        width: 300,
        height: 100,
        items: [{
            xtype: 'textfield',
            fieldLabel: 'Name',
            anchor: '90%'
        }, {
            xtype: 'numberfield',
            fieldLabel: 'Age'
        }]
    });
});
```

4. Create a file named index.html under the ch03\extjs folder and save the following code inside it:

```
<html>
<head>
    <meta http-equiv="Content-Type" content="text/html;
charset=utf-8">
    <title id="page-title">Account Manager</title>

    <link rel="stylesheet" type="text/css" href="../../extjsapp/
extjs-4.1.0-rc1/resources/css/ext-all.css">
```

```
        <script type="text/javascript" src="../../extjsapp/extjs-
4.1.0-rc1/ext-debug.js"></script>

        <script type="text/javascript" src="ch03_01.js"></script>
</head>
<body>

</body>
</html>
```

Change the path of ExtJS files based on their location on your system.

5. Run the application and look at your browser tool to see how the loader loads various files to bring up the application. The following screenshot shows the output of the **Network** tab on Chrome's developer tool:

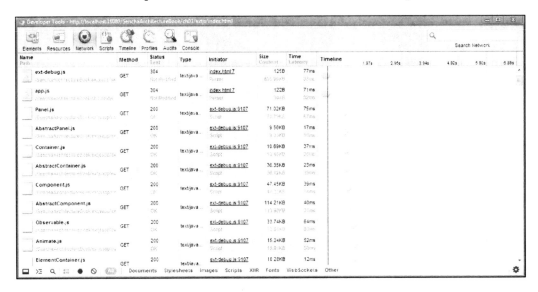

As soon as the app.js file is loaded and it tries to instantiate Panel, the loader identifies its dependencies, for example, Panel extends AbstractPanel, and it loads them immediately.

6. Create a file ch03_01.js under the ch03\touch folder and save the following code inside it:

```
Ext.setup({
  onReady: function() {
    var pnl = Ext.create('Ext.Panel', {
      fullscreen: true,
      items: [{
```

```
            xtype: 'titlebar',
              docked: 'top',
              title: 'My Panel'
        }, {
          xtype: 'textfield',
          label: 'Name'
        }, {
          xtype: 'numberfield',
          label: 'Age'
        }]
      });

      Ext.Viewport.add(pnl);
    }
  });
```

7. Create a file named `index.html` under the `ch03\touch` folder and save the following code inside it:

```html
<!DOCTYPE html PUBLIC "-//W3C//DTD HTML 4.01 Transitional//EN"
"http://www.w3.org/TR/html4/loose.dtd">
<html>
<head>
<meta http-equiv="Content-Type" content="text/html;
charset=ISO-8859-1">
<title>Account Manager</title>

<!-- Sencha Touch specific files -->
<link rel="stylesheet" type="text/css" href="../../touchapp/
sencha-touch-2.0.0/resources/css/sencha-touch.css">
<script type="text/javascript" src="../../touchapp/sencha-
touch-2.0.0/sencha-touch-debug.js"></script>

<!-- Application specific files -->
<script type="text/javascript" src="app.js"></script>

</head>
<body>

</body>
</html>
```

Change the path of Sencha Touch files based on their location on your system.

8. Run the application and look at your browser tool to see how the Loader loads various files to bring up the application. The following screenshot shows the output of the **Network** tab on Chrome's developer tool:

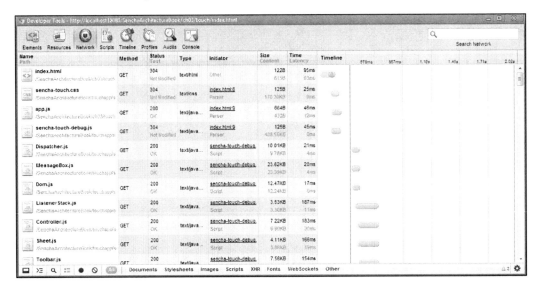

The class system offers various functionalities, which we will see in the subsequent sections.

Naming convention

The new class system has implemented various naming conventions including classes, methods, files, variables, properties, and so on. Usage of this makes the code more readable, structured, and maintainable.

Class

Class has the following properties:

- Class names contain alphanumeric characters
- Numbers are permitted but discouraged
- Use of underscores, hyphens, or any other non-alphanumeric characters is discouraged
- Class names should be grouped into packages where appropriate
- Class names should be properly namespaced using object property dot notation(.)

- The top-level namespaces and the actual class names should be camelCased. For example, `MyApp.view.user.CustomerList`

- Acronyms should also follow camelCased convention. For example,(). `Ext.data.JsonProxy`

File

While writing the code, a source file maps to a class defined inside it. As per this, one file must define a single class. For example, the `AM.view.user.List` class is stored in the `<app root src path>\view\user\List.js` file. `AM` is the namespace which maps to the application's root source folder.

Always have a separate folder for each namespace and maintain all the code within that namespace. For example, in the application that we built in the previous chapter, `AM` points to the default `app` folder. For middleware related classes, we created a new folder, `mw`, and kept the classes under the `MW` namespace.

Methods and variables

Methods and variables have the following properties:

- Method and variable names contain alphanumeric characters

- Numbers are permitted but are discouraged

- Use of underscores, hyphens, or any other non-alphanumeric characters is discouraged

- Method and variable name shall be camelCased (note that it starts with lowercase). For example, `getUserByDepartment()` or `isValid`

Properties

The class properties has the following properties:

- The naming convention that applies to methods and variables also applies to class properties other than static properties, which are constants.

- For static properties, which are constants, name, will all be upper-case. For example, `Ext.MessageBox.YES`.

Defining a class

The new class system has introduced a new method called `Ext.define` to define a new class. The following code shows how we have defined a `User` class, which has got three properties—`name`, `address`, and `age`—a constructor, and a `getName` method:

```
Ext.onReady(function() {

  //Define class
  Ext.define('User', {
    name: '',
    address: '',
    age: 0,

    constructor: function(name, address, age) {
      this.name = name;
      this.address = address;
      this.age = age;
    },
    getName: function() {
      return this.name;
    }
  });

  //Create an instance
  var user = new User('Ajit Kumar', 'Plot# 66, ABC Lane, XYZ Street,
My State, My Country - 500014', 34);

  alert(user.getName());
});
```

Once the class is defined, we used the `Ext.create` method offered by the class system to create an instance of the `User` object. Once instantiated, we can access the properties or call methods as shown in the earlier code where we are calling the `getName` method to show the username on the screen. You may save the earlier code in a file, say `ch03_02.js`, include it in `index.html` and run it in your browser to play with it.

Configuration

The previous code has a couple of issues:

* The class is defined and instantiated in the same file, whereas it should have been in a separate file

- We had to implement the getter method for the `name` property. Similarly, we may have to write explicit getter/setter methods for the other properties as the accessors. In JavaScript, every character that we add to the source, it adds to the file size and hence to the application's download time. Imagine an enterprise application with 20-50 classes, where you would like to follow the good programming practice by providing the accessor methods!

To take care of these listed problems, we will have to make some changes to our code. First, we will move the class definition to a separate file called `User.js`. So, `User.js` will have the following code:

```
Ext.define('User', {
  config: {
    name: '',
    address: '',
    age: 0
  },
  constructor: function(config) {
    this.initConfig(config);
  }
});
```

Enclose the three class properties inside `config`, as shown in the code we just used. Modify the constructor to accept a configuration object and use that to set the members using the `initConfig` method. `config` is a special property on a class, which the class system uses to automatically generate the getter and setter methods for the properties listed inside it. So, now that we have moved our properties inside the `config`, we don't have to implement the `getName()` or `getAddress()` methods. They are generated at run-time.

Now, we would modify the code where we were instantiating the class with the following:

```
Ext.onReady(function() {

  var user = Ext.create('User', {
    name: 'Ajit Kumar',
    address: 'Plot# 66, ABC Lane, XYZ Street, My State, My Country -
500014',
    age: 34
  });

  alert(user.name + ":" + user.getAddress());
});
```

Running this code would show the user's name and address.

Alias

In the previous chapter, we gave the alias names to our various view classes, for example, `widget.userlist` to `AM.view.user.List` class. Alias is another name by which the class can be referred. There are rules built into the system around this property in some cases. For example, when we defined the `widget.userlist` property as an alias, we could use `userlist` as an `xtype` and the class loader would be able to resolve the `userlist` property to `AM.view.user.List` based on the built-in rule around the `alias`.

If we give an alias to our class name it will have multiple names, and different parts of the applications can use different names but still mean the same object. Let us say, we want to give an alias name `AppUser` to our `User` class so that we can instantiate it using the alias name.

To achieve this, first, we will have to set the `alias` property on the `User` class, as shown:

```
Ext.define('User', {
  alias: ['AppUser'],
  config: {
```

Now, if we try to create the user instance using the `AppUser` name, the class loader will fail to locate the file where the `User` class is defined as it will be looking for the `AppUser.js` file, which does not exist. To address this problem, we will have to add the following statement before the `Ext.onReady()` call:

```
Ext.require('User');
```

In the previous statement, we have explicitly mentioned the dependency so that the loader loads it and once it is loaded, we are free to create the instance using the alias name as shown in the following code:

```
var user = Ext.create('AppUser', {
  name: 'Ajit Kumar',
  address: 'Plot# 66, ABC Lane, XYZ Street, My State, My Country -
500014',
  age: 34
});
```

`alias` is generally used to define as `xtype`.

Alternate class name

A class has a property—`alternateClassName`—which can be used to define any number of alternate names for the class. Once defined, the class can be referred using any of these alternate names. For example, in the following code, we have defined an alternate name `AppUser` for our `User` class as shown in the following code:

```
Ext.define('User', {
  alternateClassName: 'AppUser',
  config: {
```

Once defined, the instance of the class can be created using the alternate name, similar to how we instantiated using the `alias` name. The `Ext.require` statement must mention the `User` class if you want to use the alternate name to instantiate the class.

Extend

A class can be extended from an existing class and this is indicated using the extend property on a class. In the following code, we have defined the `Employee` class, which extends the `User` class. It defines an additional property: `department`.

```
Ext.define('Employee', {
  extend: 'User',
  config: {
    department: ''
  },
  constructor: function(config) {
    this.initConfig(config);
  }
});
```

Save this code in the `Employee.js` file for future references.

Now, we can create an instance of `Employee` by passing the properties for it, as shown in the following code:

```
var employee = Ext.create('Employee', {
  name: 'Ajit Kumar',
  address: 'Plot# 66, ABC Lane, XYZ Street, My State, My Country -
500014',
  age: 34,
  department: 'Finance'
});
```

Since we used the `config` term in the `Employee` class, the getter/setter methods are available to us and we can call them to show the employee detail by using the following command:

```
alert(employee.getName() + ":" + employee.getDepartment());
```

Statics

In a class we can define static properties as well as methods. Static properties and methods are called class-level properties and methods, which means to access them we do not need an instance object. They are accessed directly using the class.

In the following code, we modified our `User` class' definition inside `User.js` by adding a `count` static property to keep track of the number of instances created in the system, as shown in the following code:

```
statics: {
    count: 0
  },
constructor: function(config) {
    this.initConfig(config);
    this.self.count++;
  }
```

To access static properties, one has to use the `this.self` keyword, which gives the reference to the class, as we did in the `constructor` code to increment the `count` counter.

The following code shows how we can use the static property to print the number of users created in the system:

```
alert('Total users in the system: ' + User.count);
```

Inheritable statics

In case we want to inherit a static property from the parent class to the child class, we will have to use the `inheritableStatics` keyword in place of `statics`, as shown in the following code snippet:

```
inheritableStatics: {
    count: 0
  },
```

Once this change is made in the `User` class, the `count` property can be accessed inside the `Employee` class as shown in the following code snippet:

```
constructor: function(config) {
    this.initConfig(config);
    this.self.count++;
}
```

Now, we can create as many instances as we need in the application and the `count` property will keep track of them:

```
Ext.create('AppUser', {
    …
});

Ext.create('Employee', {
    …
});

Ext.create('Employee', {
    …
});

Ext.create('Employee', {
    …
});

alert('Total users in the system: ' + Employee.count);
```

When the previous code is run, it will print 4.

Mixin

Mixin is a pattern which allows us to mix one class' properties and their behavior into the other class. The classes (say, A) mentioned as mixins are merged into a class (say, B) then the properties and methods of class A can directly be accessed through class B.

Say, we want to have a method `getString` on our `User` class, which can return the string format of the object containing the user's name, age, and address. Now, we want to implement this in such a way that it can be applied to any class, which has got three properties—`name`, `address`, and `age`. So, we first define a `ToString` class with the `getString` method, as shown in the following code:

```
Ext.define('ToString', {
    getString: function() {
        return "NAME: " + this.name + "\nADDRESS: " + this.address + "\
```

```
nAGE: " + this.age;
    }
});
```

As per the naming convention, we will save the previous code in the
`ToString.js` file.

Now, we would mention the `ToString` class as a `mixin` property on the
`User` class, as shown in the following code:

```
config: {
    name: '',
    address: '',
    age: 0
},
mixins: {
    Stringyfy: 'ToString'
},
```

Mixins are, by default, inheritable. So, `getString` can be called on the `Employee`
instances, as well. However, for the employee, let us say we also want to add the
`department` info to the string. To achieve that, in the `Employee` class we will add a
`getString` method, which will call the base `getString` method of the mixin class,
that can give us the name, address, and age information, and append the department
information to it, as shown in the following code:

```
config: {
    department: ''
},
getString: function() {
    return this.mixins.Stringyfy.getString.call(this) + "\nDEPARTMENT:
" + this.department;
},
```

Now we can call the `getString` method on the user object to show the details
of the user, such as the name, address, and age by using the following command:

```
alert(user.getString());
```

We can also call the `getString` method on the employee object to show the name, address, age, and department detail of the employee by using the following command:

```
alert(employee.getString());
```

When we run the code, it shows the employee detail in the alert, as shown in the following screenshot:

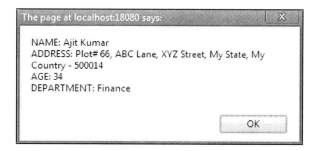

Singleton

A class has a `singleton` property which can be used to tell the framework that only one instance of the class needs to be created. For example, in the following code, we have defined a `Logger` class as a singleton, which provides a `log` method that can be used to log messages on the console:

```
Ext.define('Logger', {
    singleton: true,
    log: function(msg) {
        console.log(msg);
    }
});
```

Save this code in the `Logger.js` file for future reference.

We will have to include the `Logger` class in the `Ext.require` list so that it is loaded:

```
Ext.require(['User', 'Logger']);
```

Now, we can make use of the class and call the `log` method in the code, as shown:

```
Logger.log(employee.getString());
```

When we run the application, we can see the employee information logged on the browser console, as shown in the following screenshot:

Uses versus requires

In the earlier code, we used `Ext.require` to list down the dependencies. A similar property exists on the class `requires` which is used to list out the class dependencies. All the dependencies listed in the class `requires` are loaded before the class can be initialized. The following code shows that `Logger` is mentioned as a dependency, which is required by the `User` class to log anything:

```
Ext.define('User', {
    alias: ['AppUser'],
    requires: ['Logger'],
```

When we run the application, we can see that the `Logger.js` is being loaded right after `User.js` is loaded, as shown in the following screenshot:

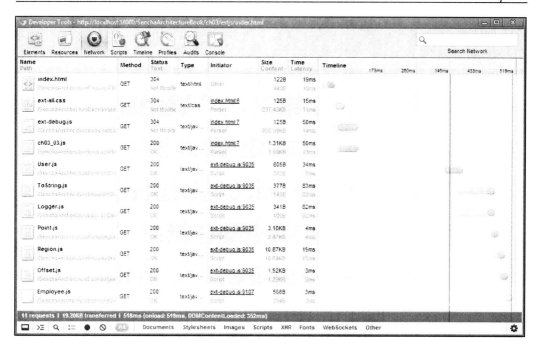

The property `uses` is available on a class to specify the classes that the class uses and it may not be a pre-requisite to the initialization of the class. If that is the case, we can use the `uses` property and list out the classes in it, as shown in the following code:

```
Ext.define('User', {
    alias: ['AppUser'],
    uses: ['Logger'],
```

In this case, the class `Logger` gets loaded before the `onReady` listener is called. The following screenshot shows that the sequence of load is different from the one in case of `requires` class:

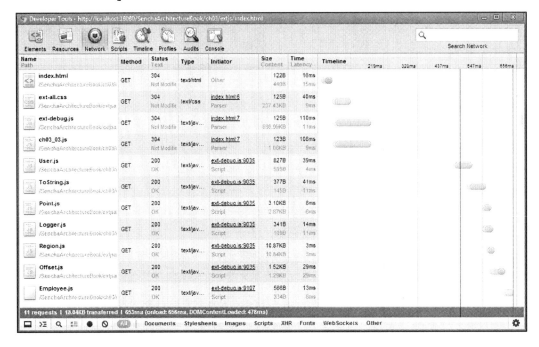

Error reporting

Error reporting is a very important aspect of an application. The better the error reporting, the better the application usage and robustness would be. In the new class system, support has been built to report errors along with the stack trace. If the new `Error` class is used, it shows a nice error trace in the browser console. So, we would replace the `alert` message that we put in the `User` class to show a message of the `age` value for a user who is less than 18 years with the following statement:

```
throw new Error('Age must be greater than 18 Years');
```

Now when a user is instantiated where the age is less than 18 years, we can see the following error trace:

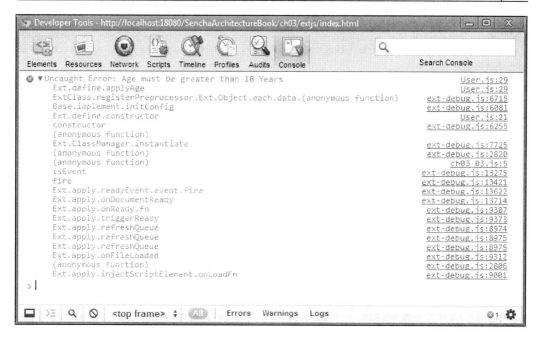

This makes the error handling and debugging a lot better. But, here is the not-so-good news. This functionality is, currently, available only on Webkit browsers.

Class loader

In *Chapter 2, Creating an Application*, we saw that we included `ext-debug.js` in the `index.html` folder, which has a smaller footprint compared to `ext-all-debug.js`. Also, as shown in the figure under the fifth item in the *Class system* section, the dependencies are automatically downloaded. This is taken care of by the class loader and hence it saves us from specifying the dependencies, manually.

The new class system has introduced a class loader, which takes care of resolving the class dependencies and loads them. This becomes very handy during the development.

The class loader functionality is provided by the `Ext.Loader` class and is enabled, by default, only when we use the development version (for example, `ext-debug.js` or `sench-touch-debug.js`) of the framework. It can be explicitly enabled by adding the following line of code before the `Ext.application` call in the `app.js` file:

```
Ext.Loader.setConfig({ enabled: true });
```

This class loader supports three types of loading:

Asynchronous loading

To tell the class loader to load the dependencies, asynchronously, the framework offers two APIs:

- `Ext.require`: This is used to list out the classes, which are required and the loader will load those classes.

  For example, `Ext.require('Ext.window.Window');`

- `Ext.exclude`: This is used to list out the classes, which are not required and the loader will skip them.

  For example, `Ext.exclude('Ext.data.*').require('*'); //Exclude data package`

The following are the advantages of asynchronous loading:

- Classes can be downloaded from the same as well as different domain
- No web server needed: You can run the application via the filesystem protocol (that is, `file://path/to/your/index .html`)
- Best possible debugging experience: Error messages come with the exact filename and line number

Following are the disadvantages of asynchronous loading:

- Dependencies need to be specified before hand

Synchronous loading

The class loader does the synchronous loading when we call `Ext.create` or `Ext.widget` to instantiate a call or a view, respectively. `Ext.create` is used to create an instance of any class in Sencha ExtJS as well as Touch whereas `Ext.widget` is used to instantiate a view using its `xtype`.

When the `Ext.create` is called, the class system checks whether the class is already present in the memory. If it is not, the loader loads the class before the class system can initialize it.

The following are the advantages of synchronous loading:

- There is no need to specify dependencies before hand

The following are the disadvantages of synchronous loading:

- Not as good a debugging experience since the file name won't be shown (except in Firebug at the moment)
- Must be from the same domain due to XHR restriction
- Need a web server as the file protocol will not work

Hybrid loading

Hybrid loading brings in the best of the synchronous and asynchronous loading. It has all the advantages combined from synchronous and asynchronous loading.

As an approach, we will start with synchronous loading, and to have a better debugging experience, we would use the asynchronous loading. There are other ways to make the debugging experience better, which we will see in the next chapter.

Also, the dynamic loading shall be used during the development. In production, we must be using the minified version so that all the dependencies are combined in a single file. loader.

Summary

In this chapter, we looked into how the new class system works and what are the functionalities offered by the class system. We also saw what are the naming conventions put in place and recommended by the framework, how to define classes, set up dependencies, implement inheritance, enhance capability using mixins, create singleton classes, and so on. In the next chapter, we will see what kind of development and deployment challenges the new class system presents in front of us and how we tackle them.

5

Challenges and Solutions

In the previous chapters, we developed an MVC application for Ext JS as well as Sencha Touch frameworks, where we used the dynamic class loading capability of the loader, which is part of the new class system, to ensure that we did not have to include all the JS files in the `index.html` folder. Still the required classes are loaded and the classes were initialized properly. Well, while that sounds like a great thing, it introduces a few development challenges. For example, we know that we would not like to release the source files as they are, in production. So, is there a way that we can package the source files for production deployment?

In this chapter, we will look at the main challenges and see how to solve them.

Challenges

In this section, we will look at some of the major challenges—creating a project, debugging, packaging, and deploying—in creating an MVC application using Sencha MVC architecture.

Project creation

Though we discussed about a folder structure for a Sencha MVC-based application development, in *Chapter 2, Creating an Application,* it is generally better if this process is automated so that we can ensure the consistency across the projects, and also give scope for further automation.

Debugging

In the previous chapter, we learnt about the loader's synchronous and asynchronous mode of loading the scripts. Based on whether we use the `<srcipt>` tag, or `Ext.require`, or `requires`, or `Ext.create`, or `xtype`, the class loader loads the class scripts synchronously or asynchronously. When we developed our MVC applications, we used the combination of `Ext.require`, `requires`, `Ext.create`, and `xtype`. Only `app.js` was included in the `index.html`.

Say, we wanted to understand what the controller objects look like when the handler for the `itemclick` event is being registered inside the control method of the `Department` controller. We add a breakpoint on line **15** of the `app\controller\Departments.js` file, shown as follows:

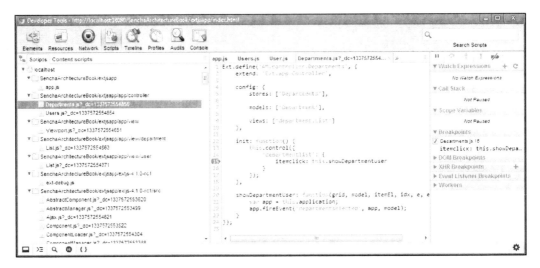

You can refer to `https://developers.google.com/chrome-developer-tools/docs/overview` for more detail on how to use Chrome's developer tool and how to add breakpoints.

Now hit *F5* to reload the URL and you will notice that the application has loaded and the view is rendered, but the debugger did not stop on line **15** where we had added the breakpoint. This is because of the extra parameter, `_dc`, added in the URL. The value for `_dc` is a timestamp, which is generated each time a URL is being constructed. Due to this, the browser always downloads the file freshly from the server. From the development perspective, not being able to debug the code is a big problem as it may put pressure on the timeline and the overall quality of the deliverables. In the *Solution*, section of this chapter, we will see how to address this.

Build

The default project setup that we had created and used in the previous chapters, loaded all the dependencies from the source files. The code was well formatted along with the comments. This is acceptable in a development environment. However, in production, you would not like to deploy the source files unless that is part of your licensing model. This way you would expose your implementation to the outside world and bear the consequences of that. Though there is no way that we can avoid making our code available in the client browser, using the approach of merging the source files and obfuscating it, we can make it difficult for someone to understand the application logic. In addition to this, the merged file will also boost the initial loading time of the application as we reduce the number of files that need to be downloaded and also, the size of the minified file is much smaller as compared to the total size of the individual script files.

Now, if we were launch the extjsapp file and look at the **Scripts** tab, we would see tons of JS files being downloaded for the application to work. Now, it would be tedious to list all those files and create a build script to combine all those classes and package them together. Sencha offers tools to take care of this, where it can create a build file out of an existing application, which can later be used with a build tool to build the project.

Minification

The challenge that we had with the build where we had to manage so many files, which get downloaded to initialize the application and make it functional, applies to the minification process as well. Minification is a very important task in any JavaScript project as it combines all the source code, removes extra space, new lines, and tabs to create a file with a smaller footprint. This helps us reduce the loading time for the code.

We will see what tools Sencha offers to take care of the minification so that we are able to release a production-ready application.

Solutions

Now that we have listed out our problems in the previous section, let us see what Sencha offers to address them.

The solution suggested here will work for Ext JS as well as Sencha Touch. However, wherever the solution is specific to a particular framework, it will be mentioned.

Project creation

Sencha provides an SDK tool to help us in managing the lifecycle of project development. One of the tasks it helps us with is the automatic creation of the project's folder structure and the files needed to get a basic MVC-based application created. The generated code can be deployed and run without any changes. But before we do anything, we need to get the Sencha SDK tool installed on our system.

The following are the steps to install the SDK tool:

1. Download and install the Sencha Ext JS framework.
2. Download and install the Sencha Touch framework.
3. Download and install the SDK tool from `http://www.sencha.com/products/sdk-tools/`.
4. Add the `/path/to/sdk-tools/bin` folder to the path. Once this is done, the tool can be run from anywhere in your filesystem.
5. Go to `/path/to/sencha-touch-framework`. This is required as the tool picks up the Sencha framework from the current directory where the command is being run.

6. Run **sencha help** on the command prompt. It will show you the following output:

```
c:\xampp\htdocs\sencha-touch-2.0.0-gpl>"C:\Program Files (x86)\SenchaSDKTools-2.0.0-beta3\sencha" help
Sencha Command v2.0.0 for Sencha Touch 2
Copyright (c) 2012 Sencha Inc.

Usage:
    sencha [module] [action] [arguments...]

Example:
    sencha fs minify --from app.js --to app-minified.js --compressor closurecompiler

Available modules:

    app          Resolve application dependencies and build for production
    fs           A set of useful utility actions to work with files. Most commonly used actions are: concat, minify, delta
    manifest     Extract class metadata
    test         Unit testing using Jasmine
    generate     Automates the generation of projects and files
    package      Packages a Sencha Touch 2 application for native app stores

For more information on a specific module, simply type:
    sencha [module]

For example:
    sencha fs

For more information on a specific action of a specific module, simply type:
    sencha [module] [action]

For example:
    sencha fs minify
```

7. Go to `/path/to/sencha-extjs-framework`.

8. Run **sencha help** on the command prompt. It will show you the following output:

```
c:\xampp\htdocs\extjs-4.1.0-rc1>"C:\Program Files (x86)\SenchaSDKTools-2.0.0-beta1\sencha" help
[WARN] The current working directory (c:\xampp\htdocs\extjs-4.1.0-rc1) is not a recognized Sencha SDK or application folder. Running in backwards compatible mode.

Sencha Command v2.0.0 Beta 3
Copyright (c) 2012 Sencha Inc.

usage: sencha COMMAND [ARGS]

The available commands are:
build                    build a JSB project
    create bootstrapdata     generate boostrap data
    create jsb               generate a minimal JSB project for an app
    create locale            generate a template locale file from source
    create manifest          generate classes manifest
    package                  package your Touch web app into a native bundle
    slice theme              slice a custom theme's images for IE

See 'sencha help COMMAND' for more information on a specific command.
```

Notice that the Ext JS part does not have the `generate target` function, which is available for Touch. This means that the SDK tool currently does not have the support to generate an Ext JS-based project skeleton. We hope this will soon be supported in the tool!

Now that we have installed the SDK tool, creating a new Sencha Touch project is as simple as running the following command:

```
sencha generate app -n AM -p c:\senchalab\ profile -n desktop
```

The previous command will create a Sencha Touch 2 application with the name AM, and generate the view class for the desktop profile, shown as follows:

In addition to the project's folder structure and the standard app.js and index. html, the tool generates the following files and folders to support the build and packaging:

- app.json: This is used by the build tool to build the project and create the <app>-all.js and <app>-all-debug.js files.

- packager.json: This is used by the tool to create native packages for different devices like Android, iOS, and so on.

- .senchasdk: This contains the folder where the Touch framework resides. It defaults to sdk. But in case your Touch framework related files are in a different folder, you can change this file to point it to that folder.

- resources\icons: This contains different icons used for applications on different devices and resolutions. By default, it contains the Sencha icons that you may have to replace with your application-specific icons.

- resources\loading: This contains icons used to display at the time of loading of the application. By default, it contains the Sencha icons that you may have to replace with your application-specific icons.

- resources\sass: This contains the theme-related files that can be used to generate different themes for our application.

The project thus generated can be deployed and run without any modification. For example, I moved it inside my `htdocs` folder on the web server and I got the following output when I accessed it from the browser:

Now that the basic project skeleton is done, we can start making changes to it to make it an enterprise application.

Debugging

By default, the loader appends the timestamp while loading a class, and due to that, the files are not cached and the debugging at the time of loading becomes impossible. For example, we wanted to know what the controller object looks like when we registers the `itemclick` event on a view inside the `control` method of the `Department` controller. To achieve this, we can do the following:

User <script> tag

Include the `Department` controller file — `Departments.js` — into the `index.html` file by adding the following line:

```
<script type="text/javascript" src="app/controller/Departments.js"></
script>
```

Deploy and run the application. Now, you will see that the _dc parameter is not appended to the `Departments.js` controller file and the debugger stops at the breakpoint, shown as follows:

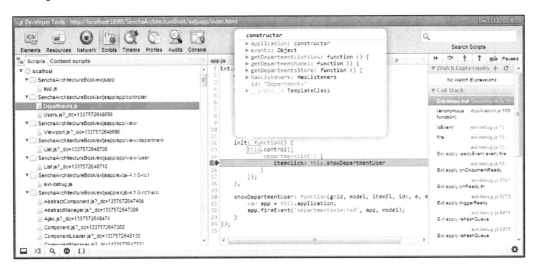

Disable caching for loader

In the previous approach, you had to list out the files in the `index.html`. However, this may not be desirable as you may not know what files you would like to debug at the runtime. If this is the case, we need a different approach. The `Ext.Loader` class implements the class loading. It has a property—`disableCaching`—which is, by default, `true`. That means, by default, the loader appends a timestamp while loading a file and due to that they are not cached. To disable the caching for all the files used in the application, we will have to set the configuration on the loader, shown as follows:

```
Ext.Loader.setConfig({
   disableCaching: false
});
```

Add these lines of code in the `app.js` file, just before the `Ext.application` call. Now, when you run the application, you can see that the `_dc` parameter is not appended to the files, shown as follows:

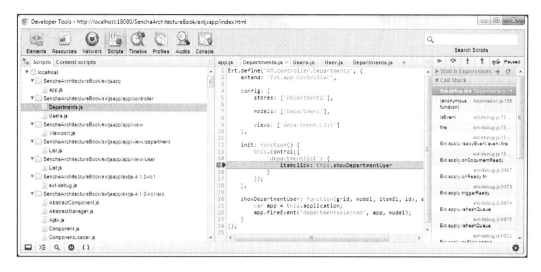

Build

Sencha has provided a tool called **JSBuilder** to build JavaScript projects. It is supported by the SDK tools. The JSBuilder expects a `.jsb` file to be provided to it, which is a JSON file containing the project configuration and the files that need to be considered in the build to create the package. The current version of JSBuilder is 3 and the file extension is `.jsb3`. The SDK tool provides a convenient target to generate the `jsb3` file from an existing project. For example, to generate the `jsb3` file for the `extjsapp` project that we had created in *Chapter 2, Creating an Application*, we will have to do the following:

1. Deploy the application and run the server.

2. Run the following command:

```
sencha create jsb -a http://localhost:18080/
SenchaArchitectureBook/extjsapp/index.html -p c:\workspace\
SenchaArchitectureBook\WebContent\extjsapp\extjsapp.jsb3
```

After the command exits, we can see an `extjsapp.jsb3` file created in our project's root folder, shown as follows:

The tool produces the defaults and we may want to change some of them. For example, we changed the `projectName`, `licenseText`, and target for `All Classes` that is used to create the package when the target is built by modifying these fields inside the `extjsapp.jsb3` file, shown as follows:

```
 1 {
 2     "projectName": "ExtJS MVC App",
 3     "licenseText": "Copyright(c) 2012 Walking Tree Consultancy Services Pvt. Ltd.",
 4     "builds": [
 5         {
 6             "name": "All Classes",
 7             "target": "extjsapp-all-debug.js",
 8             "options": {
 9                 "debug": true
10             },
11             "files": [
```

Also, change the detail for the `Application-Production` target and include the `app.js` file:

```
979         {
980             "name": "Application - Production",
981             "target": "extjsapp-all.js",
982             "compress": true,
983             "files": [
984                 {
985                     "path": "",
986                     "name": "extjsapp-all-debug.js"
987                 },
988                 {
989                     "path": "",
990                     "name": "app.js"
991                 }
992             ]
993         }
```

 Notice that the `Application-Production` target includes the `app.js` file, whereas `All Classes` does not.

Now that the `jsb3` file is created, we can use it to build and package our application by running the following command:

```
sencha build -p c:\workspace\SenchaArchitectureBook\WebContent\extjsapp\
extjsapp.jsb3 -d c:\workspace\SenchaArchitectureBook\WebContent\extjsapp\
```

This command will build the project as per the `jsb3` file and create two files:

- `extjsapp-all.js`: This contains the required classes, obfuscated, and compressed

- `extjsapp-all-debug.js`: This contains the required classes

app	26-04-2012 08:26 ...	File folder	
data	26-04-2012 08:26 ...	File folder	
extjs-4.1.0-rc1	26-04-2012 08:27 ...	File folder	
app.js	20-05-2012 04:52 ...	JS File	1 KB
extjsapp.jsb3	20-05-2012 05:41 ...	JSB3 File	37 KB
extjsapp-all.js	20-05-2012 05:42 ...	JS File	588 KB
extjsapp-all-debug.js	20-05-2012 05:42 ...	JS File	2,533 KB
index.html	20-05-2012 04:50 ...	HTML File	1 KB

Now, we modify the `index.html` file to include `extjsapp-all.js` (since it contains `app.js` also) in place of `app.js`, shown as follows:

```
<html>
<head>
  <meta http-equiv="Content-Type" content="text/html; charset=utf-8">
  <title id="page-title">Account Manager</title>

  <link rel="stylesheet" type="text/css" href="extjs-4.1.0-rc1/
resources/css/ext-all.css">
  <script type="text/javascript" src="extjs-4.1.0-rc1/ext-debug.js"></
script>
  <script type="text/javascript" src="extjsapp-all.js"></script>

</head>
<body>

</body>
</html>
```

In case you use `extjsapp-all-debug.js`, you will have to include `app.js` as well in your `index.html`.

Run the application. The application works as before but we see very few files being loaded on the **Scripts** tab of the browser's developer tool, shown as follows:

Notice that, the model classes and store classes are still being loaded separately. When we look into the generated `jsb3` file, the entries are not there. So, we will add them by adding the following code before the controller files inside the `extjsapp.jsb3` file:

```
{
  "clsName": "AM.model.User",
  "name": "User.js",
  "path": "app/model/"
},
{
  "clsName": "AM.model.Department",
  "name": "Department.js",
  "path": "app/model/"
},
{
  "clsName": "AM.store.Users",
  "name": "Users.js",
  "path": "app/store/"
},
{
  "clsName": "AM.store.Departments",
```

```
    "name": "Departments.js",
    "path": "app/store/"
},
```

Build and run the application again. Now, you will not see the separate loads for the model and store classes, shown as follows:

Though the tool tries its best to take care of the things, there may be situations where you may have to make some changes. And given what we have discussed, we know what change needs to be done in which place.

The SDK tool provides an additional capability for Sencha Touch-based applications where we can do native packaging of our application. This is kept outside the scope of the book as it has been described in the API documentation under the **Guides** tab. The following are some of the relevant URLs:

- Native packaging for Android: `http://docs.sencha.com/touch/2-0/#!/guide/native_android`

- Native packaging for iOS: `http://docs.sencha.com/touch/2-0/#!/guide/native_packaging`

Minification

With SDK Tools, we don't have to do anything additional to get the source minified. It is the integral part of the build process and is driven by the compress property on the target configuration inside the `jsb3` file. When it is set to true, the tool creates the minified output.

Summary

In this chapter, we looked at some of the main challenges when it comes to developing an MVC based application—project creation, build, debugging, and packaging. With the challenges at hand, we then looked at the Sencha SDK tools to see how it can help us to address each of those challenges.

We started our journey with the MVC concept and how they are mapped to the Sencha MVC architecture in Ext JS as well as Sencha Touch frameworks. We then moved on to applying those concepts to see how we define a controller, view, model, stores, and so on to get a working application in Ext JS as well as Touch. After that we delved deeper into the framework classes which offer the MVC functionality and understood what goes inside when we use them in the application. Next, we learnt about the new class system introduced by the framework, what it offers, and how they work together to help us build complex and scalable applications, that are still maintainable. We looked at the loader class to see how it utilizes the dependencies to load the required classes and ensures that they are available before a class can be initialized. Lastly, in this chapter, we reviewed the challenges and addressed them using the Sencha SDK tools.

For further reading, refer to the API documentation, guides, and videos from Sencha.

Index

Symbols

(X)HTML 10

A

AbstractComponent class 74
alias, class system 82
Apache Tomcat
  ExtJS-based application, publishing 40, 41
  Sencha Touch-based application,
    publishing 53, 54
application
  demo page 24
application design
  about 25
  controllers 27
  datafiles 26
  ExtJS-based application 27
  models 25
  Sencha Touch-based application 41
  stores 25
  views 25
asynchronous loading 92
autoCreateViewport:true property 39

B

beginEdit operation 61
building blocks, Sencha Ext JS/Touch
  about 58
  controllers 65
  model 58
  view 64

C

caching for loader
  disabling 102
cancelEdit operation 61
challenges, MVC application
  build 96
  debugging 95, 96
  minification 98
  project creation 95
changedWhileEditing operation 61
class
  configuration 80
  defining, in class system 80
classes, ExtJS-based application
  Ext.app.Application 27
  Ext.app.Controller 27
  Ext.container.Container 27
  Ext.data.Model 27
  Ext.data.Store 27
classes, Sencha Touch-based application
  Ext.app.Application 41
  Ext.app.Controller 41
  Ext.Component 41
  Ext.Container 41
  Ext.data.Model 42
  Ext.data.Store 42
Class loader
  about 91
  asynchronous loading 92
  hybrid loading 93
  synchronous loading 92, 93
class, naming conventions
  properties 78

class properties, naming conventions 79
class system
  requires class, using 88, 89
Class System
  about 74
  alias 82
  alternate class name 83
  class, defining 80
  class hierarchy 74
  error reporting 90
  extend property 83
  inheritable statics 84, 85
  Mixin 85, 86
  naming conventions 78
  singleton property 87
  static properties 84
  UI, creating 75, 76, 78
Client-side MVC architecture
  features 10, 12
commit operation 60
controller
  about 65
  in, Ext JS framework 65
  in, Touch framework 65
controller, ExtJS-based application folder
      structure
  about 36
  departments 38
  users 36, 37
controllers, application design
  departments 27
  users 27
controller, Sencha Touch-based application
      folder structure
  about 50
  departments 51, 52
  users 50, 51
convertDeptCodeToName method 71
copy operation 60
CSS 10

D

datafiles, application design
  departments.json 26
  users.json 26

DataView component 17
departments.json datafile 26
destroy operation 60
Destruction phase, view 65
disableCaching 102

E

editing operation, model instance
  beginEdit 61
  cancelEdit 61
  changedWhileEditing 61
  endEdit 61
  getChanges 61
  isModified 61
endEdit operation 61
erase operation 60
error reporting 90, 91
estjsapp applications
  models, defining 58
  store, defining 61
Ext.app.Application class
  about 20, 21, 27, 41
  functionalities, in EXT JS 69
  functionalities, in Sencha Touch 69
Ext.app.Controller class 20, 21, 27, 41
Ext.app.Profile class 21
Ext.Component class 20, 21, 41
Ext.Container class 21, 41
Ext.container.Container class 20, 27
Ext.data.Model class 20, 21, 27, 42
Ext.data.Store class 21, 27, 42
Ext.define class 71
Ext JS
  Ext.app.Application class 69
Ext JS 4.1 20
ExtJS-based application
  about 27
  folder structure 27
  initializing 39
  publishing, to Apache Tomcat 40, 41
Ext JS framework
  controller 65
Ext.onReady method 15, 20

F

FieldAncestor mixin 74
file, naming conventions 79
filterUsersByDepartment method 31
folder structure, ExtJS-based application
  about 27
  application 38, 39
  controller 36
  index.html file 39
  model 29
  store 30
  view 32
folder structure, Sencha Touch-based application
  about 42
  application 52
  controller 50
  index.html 53
  model 43
  store 44
  view 46

G

getAddress() method 81
getChanges operation 61
getName() method 81
getString method 85
getUserByDepartment() 79

H

history support, Sencha Touch 70
hybrid loading 93

I

index.html, ExtJS-based application folder structure 39
index.html file, Sencha Touch-based application folder structure 53
inheritableStatics keyword 84
initConfig method 81
Initialization phase, view 64
isModified operation 61
itemclick event 101
itemdblclick handler 17

J

JavaScript 10
JSBuilder
  about 103
  working 103-105

L

LineSegment class 74
list route 70
load operation 60, 63

M

method and variable names, naming conventions 79
mixin, class system 85, 86
model
  about 58
  defining, in estjsapp applications 58
  defining, in touchapp applications 59
  Department 58
  store 61
  User 58
model class
  fields 59, 60
model, ExtJS-based application folder structure
  about 29
  department 30
  user 30
model instance
  editing operations 61
  operations 60
models, application design
  department 25
  user 25
model, Sencha Touch-based application folder structure
  about 43
  department 44
  user 44
MVC application
  challenges 95
  solution 98

MVC architecture
  about 7
  diagrammatic representation 10

N

naming conventions, class system
  about 78
  class 78
  file 79
  properties 79
Native packaging for Android
  URL 107
Native packaging for iOS
  URL 107

O

Observable class 74
operations, model instance
  commit 60
  copy 60
  destroy 60
  erase 60
  load 60
  reject 60
  save 60
  validate 60
operations, store instance
  load 63
  sync 63

P

profile, Sencha Touch 66
property, class system 83, 84

R

reject operation 60
Render phase, view 64
Rich Internet Applications (RIA) 11
routing, Sencha Touch 70

S

save operation 60
SenchaArchitectureBook project set up
  steps 7-9

Sencha Ext JS/Touch
  about 18
  building blocks 58
  diagrammatic representation 18
Sencha MVC architecture
  about 18, 19
  benefits 18
  building blocks 58
  Class loader 91
  Class System 73, 74
  Ext JS 4.1 20
  features 12-17
  Loader 73
  Sencha Touch 21
Sencha SDK tool
  downloading 98
  installing 98, 99
Sencha Touch
  about 21
  components 21
  controller 65
  dependency management, with loader 71,
    72
  Ext.app.Application class 69
  history support 70
  profile 66-68
  routing 70
Sencha Touch-based application
  about 41
  folder structure 42
  publishing, to Apache Tomcat 53, 54
showUsersByDepartment method 70
showUsersList method 70
singleton property, class system 87
solution, MVC application
  build 103
  debugging 101
  minification 108
  project creation 98-100
static properties, class system
  about 84
  inheritable statics 84, 85
store
  about 61
  autoLoad 63
  autoSync 63
  defining, in estjsapp applications 61

defining, in touchapp applications 62
fields 62
store, ExtJS-based application folder structure
departments 32
users 30, 31
store instance
operations 63
stores, application design
departments 25
users 25
store, Sencha Touch-based application folder structure
about 44
departments 45, 46
users 44, 45
synchronous loading 92, 93
sync operation 63

T

ToString class 85
touchapp applications
models, defining 59
store, defining 62
Touch framework
controller 65

U

UI, class system
creating 75-78
user <script> tag 101
users/:id route 70
users.json datafile 26

V

validate() method 59
validate operation 60
validations config property 59
view
about 64
Destruction phase 65
Initialization phase 64
Render phase 64
view, ExtJS-based application folder structure
about 32
department list 35
user edit 33, 34
user list 32, 33
viewport 35
views, application design
edit user 25
user list 25
view, Sencha Touch-based application folder structure
about 46
department list 49
user edit 47, 48
user list 46, 47

Thank you for buying
Sencha MVC Architecture

About Packt Publishing

Packt, pronounced 'packed', published its first book "*Mastering phpMyAdmin for Effective MySQL Management*" in April 2004 and subsequently continued to specialize in publishing highly focused books on specific technologies and solutions.

Our books and publications share the experiences of your fellow IT professionals in adapting and customizing today's systems, applications, and frameworks. Our solution based books give you the knowledge and power to customize the software and technologies you're using to get the job done. Packt books are more specific and less general than the IT books you have seen in the past. Our unique business model allows us to bring you more focused information, giving you more of what you need to know, and less of what you don't.

Packt is a modern, yet unique publishing company, which focuses on producing quality, cutting-edge books for communities of developers, administrators, and newbies alike. For more information, please visit our website: www.packtpub.com.

About Packt Open Source

In 2010, Packt launched two new brands, Packt Open Source and Packt Enterprise, in order to continue its focus on specialization. This book is part of the Packt Open Source brand, home to books published on software built around Open Source licences, and offering information to anybody from advanced developers to budding web designers. The Open Source brand also runs Packt's Open Source Royalty Scheme, by which Packt gives a royalty to each Open Source project about whose software a book is sold.

Writing for Packt

We welcome all inquiries from people who are interested in authoring. Book proposals should be sent to author@packtpub.com. If your book idea is still at an early stage and you would like to discuss it first before writing a formal book proposal, contact us; one of our commissioning editors will get in touch with you.

We're not just looking for published authors; if you have strong technical skills but no writing experience, our experienced editors can help you develop a writing career, or simply get some additional reward for your expertise.

Ext JS 4 Web Application Development Cookbook

ISBN: 978-1-84951-686-0   Paperback: 488 pages

Over 110 easy-to-follow recipes backed up with real-life examples, walking you through basic Ext JS features to advanced application design using Sencha's Ext JS

1. Learn how to build Rich Internet Applications with the latest version of the Ext JS framework in a cookbook style

2. From creating forms to theming your interface, you will learn the building blocks for developing the perfect web application

3. Easy to follow recipes step through practical and detailed examples which are all fully backed up with code, illustrations, and tips

Sencha Touch Cookbook

ISBN: 978-1-84951-544-3   Paperback: 350 pages

Over 100 recipes for creating HTML5-based cross-platform apps for touch devices

1. Master cross platform application development

2. Incorporate geo location into your apps

3. Develop native looking web apps

Please check **www.PacktPub.com** for information on our titles

Sencha Touch Mobile JavaScript Framework

ISBN: 978-1-84951-510-8   Paperback: 316 pages

Build web applications for Apple iOS and Google Android touchscreen devices with this first HTML5 mobile framework

1. Learn to develop web applications that look and feel native on Apple iOS and Google Android touchscreen devices using Sencha Touch through examples

2. Design resolution-independent and graphical representations like buttons, icons, and tabs of unparalleled flexibility

3. Add custom events like tap, double tap, swipe, tap and hold, pinch, and rotate

Learning Ext JS 4

ISBN: 978-1-84951-684-6   Paperback: 504 pages

Sencha Ext JS for a beginner

1. Learn the basics and create your first classes

2. Handle data and understand the way it works, create powerful widgets and new components

3. Dig into the new architecture defined by Sencha and work on real world projects

Please check **www.PacktPub.com** for information on our titles

CPSIA information can be obtained at www.ICGtesting.com
Printed in the USA
LVOW111933141112

307344LV00004B/32/P